Research and Statistics in Physical Education

Dr. Amit Banerjee
B.P.E., M.P.E., M.Phil., Ph.D., P.G.D.S.M., C.C.Y.,
Kinanthropometry (Level - I), UGC-NET, WB-SET
Assistant Professor
Post-Graduate Government Institute for Physical Education,
Banipur, North 24 Parganas,
West Bengal

CRESCENT
PUBLISHING CORPORATION

Research and Statistics in Physical Education

Edition :2023

ISBN 978-81-8342-473-8

Published by :

CRESCENT PUBLISHING CORPORATION
4806/24, Mathur Lane,
Ansari Road, Darya Ganj,
New Delhi - 110002
Phone : 011- 23244131
Mob. : 9711991838, 9999021668
Website : www.crescentpublishingcorp.weebly.com
E-mail : crescentbook@gmail.com

Typesetting by :

Adee Computers
Delhi

Printed at :
G. S. Offset
Delhi

CONTENTS

UNIT 1: INTRODUCTION TO RESEARCH	**1-36**
1. Definition of Research	1
2. Need and Importance of Research in Physical Education and Sports	6
3. Scope of Research in Physical Education and Sports	10
4. Classification of Research	14
5. Research Problem, Meaning of the Term, Location and Criteria of Selection of Problem, Formulation of a Research Problem, Limitations and Delimitations	27
UNIT II: SURVEY OF RELATED LITERATURE	**37-83**
6. Need for Surveying Related Literature	37
7. Literature Sources, Library Reading	47
8. Research Proposal, Meaning and Significance of Research Proposal	61
9. Preparation of Research Proposal/Project	71
10. Research Report	77
UNIT III: BASICS OF STATISTICAL ANALYSIS	**84-123**
11. Statistics: Meaning, Definition, Nature and Importance	84

12. Class Intervals: Raw Score, Continuous and Discrete Series, Class Distribution, Construction of Tables 91

13. Graphical Presentation of Class Distribution: Histogram, Frequency Polygon, Frequency Curve. Cumulative Frequency Polygon, Ogive, Pie Diagram 102

UNIT IV: STATISTICAL MODELS IN PHYSICAL EDUCATION AND SPORTS 124-155

14. Measures of Central Tendency: Mean, Median and Mode-Meaning, Definition, Importance, Advantages, Disadvantages and Calculation from Group and Ungrouped Data 124

15. Measures of Variability: Meaning, Importance, Computing from Group and Ungroup Data 136

16. Percentiles and Quartiles: Meaning, Importance, Computing from Group and Ungroup Data 145

SYLLABUS

RESEARCH AND STATISTICS IN PHYSICAL EDUCATION

UNIT 1: INTRODUCTION TO RESEARCH

1. Definition of Research
2. Need and Importance of Research in Physical Education and Sports
3. Scope of Research in Physical Education and Sports
4. Classification of Research
5. Research Problem, Meaning of the Term, Location and Criteria of Selection of Problem, Formulation of a Research Problem, Limitations and Delimitations

UNIT II: SURVEY OF RELATED LITERATURE

6. Need for Surveying Related Literature
7. Literature Sources, Library Reading
8. Research Proposal, Meaning and Significance of Research Proposal
9. Preparation of Research Proposal/Project
10. Research Report

UNIT III: BASICS OF STATISTICAL ANALYSIS

11. Statistics: Meaning, Definition, Nature and Importance
12. Class Intervals: Raw Score, Continuous and Discrete Series, Class Distribution, Construction of Tables
13. Graphical Presentation of Class Distribution: Histogram, Frequency Polygon, Frequency Curve. Cumulative Frequency Polygon, Ogive, Pie Diagram

UNIT IV: STATISTICAL MODELS IN PHYSICAL EDUCATION AND SPORTS

14. Measures of Central Tendency: Mean, Median and Mode-Meaning, Definition, Importance, Advantages, Disadvantages and Calculation from Group and Ungrouped Data
15. Measures of Variability: Meaning, Importance, Computing from Group and Ungroup Data
16. Percentiles and Quartiles: Meaning, Importance, Computing from Group and Ungroup Data

UNIT 1
Introduction to Research

1

Definition of Research

Research is a human activity based on intellectual investigation and aimed at discovering, interpreting, and revising human knowledge on different aspects of the world. Research can use the scientific method, but need not do so. The term research is also used to describe an entire collection of information about a particular subject.

It is a human quest of knowledge Research is nothing but, searching or investigating new things, or new facts or new concepts or new principles or new theories. It can also be considered as the expansion of horizon of knowledge for the betterment of human life or it is a more systematic activity that is directed toward discovery and development of an organized body of knowledge.

Research - 'Any honest attempt to study a problem systematically or to add to man's knowledge of a problem may be regarded as research'.

Research is a systematic process of discovery and advancement of human knowledge.

Research is considered to be the more forma, systematic and intensive process of carrying on a scientific method of analysis.

The word research derives from the French recherche, from rechercher, to search closely where "chercher" means "to search", its literal meaning is 'to investigate thoroughly'.

The term research consists of two words,

Research = Re + Search

'Re' means again and again and 'Search' means to analyse something.

Etymologically, it means seeking the solutions to the questions or to find answers to the questions. This urge of the human brain to examine and re-examine and to understand and re-understand things may rightly be called research.

Research in physical education is the study of man as an individual engaging his motor abilities. Physical education is completely associated with the well being of man's total organism, his physical fitness, mental alertness, personal and social adjustment and emotional stability. The concept of research is closely liked with human endeavor for better understanding of the environment and growth. Strictly speaking, research is search for facts.

Research is an art of scientific investigation. It is regarded as a systematic effort to gain new knowledge. It is a "self-directed effort (Cicciarilla,1997) at finding truthful answers to questions of vital importance to man and the society. The Webster New International Dictionary explains the term research as a "careful inquiry or examination in seeking facts or principles; a diligent investigation to ascertain something." In common parlance, research is a formal work undertaken systematically to expand the universe of knowledge, including knowledge of humanity, culture and society, and the use of this stock of knowledge to devise new applications. It is used to establish or confirm facts, reaffirm results of the previous work, solve new or existing problems, support theorem, or develop new theories. Expressions such as "an attitude of mind," "systematic scholarly application of scientific methods," "systematic solution of problems," "honest, intelligence and exhaustive search for facts," "the quest for the unknown and for more about the known to reveal the secrets of the universe," etc., denote what research stands for. In sum, asking of a good question is the beginning of all research.

'Research is to see what everybody else has seen, and to think what nobody else has thought,' says Albert Szent-Gyorgi. In reality, it is an act of studying something (phenomenon) carefully and extensively in order to attain deeper knowledge about it. According to Best (1983) research is "the formal, systematic, intensive process of carrying on the scientific method of analysis." It results in some sort of formal record of procedures and a report of well churned-out results or conclusions. It offers dependable solutions to problems when systematic procedures of data collection, analysis and interpretation are applied. For some people, research is 'a diligent and systematic enquiry or investigation into a subject in order to discover, or revise facts, theories or applications'. It leads to discoveries, inventions e.g., penicillin, automobile, computer.

Research is aimed at finding the conditions under which a certain phenomenon occurs and the conditions under which it does not occur in what might appear to be similar circumstances. As an intellectual process, it is "an endeavour to discover, develop and verify knowledge," argued Rummel. Research is nothing new but has existed since the birth of civilization or even earlier - always refining its techniques of generating verifiable facts. In formal sense of the term, research is "systematic and objective analysis and recording of controlled observations that may lead to the development of generalizations, principles and theories, resulting in prediction and possibly ultimate control of events."

In its simplest sense, research is a relentless pursuit after scientific truth i.e. a vigorous search after facts. It sis a "systematic investigation (i.e. the gathering and analysis of information) designed to develop or contribute to generalizable knowledge." Oft times, this search is painful because the truth that research bares is unpopular and unpalatable for many. On this, Cicciarella (1997) remarks: "Those who speak the truth or what they honestly believe to be truth sometimes risk vilification, ridicule, loss of security, loss of professional reputation, and even serious physical harm, especially when their statements threaten widely or deeply held views or undermine established institutions."

In final analysis, research may be defined as an organized and systematic way of finding answers to questions that arise in our mind as we look around and observe things happening. When analysed, this terse statement, reveals several interesting facts. For instance, research is systematic because there is a definite set of procedures and steps which the researchers have to follow. In research process certain things are pre-requisites; without them most accurate results are difficult to obtain. Research is an organized and a meticulously planned procedure - neither a spontaneous nor a haphazard one. It is well focused and limited to a specific scope. Research ends up in finding answers to questions, which could be hypotheses or simple questions. This is the success story of research. Even if the answer, sometimes, is no, but it is still an answer. Questions are central to research. In the absence of a question, there is no attempt to find an answer. Research is focused on relevant, useful, and important questions. Without a question, research has neither any focus, nor drive, nor any purpose.

CHARACTERSTICS OF RESEARCH

With the help of the definitions of research we can arrive at the following characteristics.

1. Research is always directed towards the solution of a problem.
2. Research demands accurate observations and description. It is not merely a collection of data or information.
3. Research requires the collection of first hand information or the data from the primary sources.
4. Research should have carefully designed systematic procedure by applying advance analysis of resultant date.
5. Research should possess complete knowledge in the area of investigation.
6. Research requires a logical, critical and objective approach in problem solving.
7. Research should be carefully recorded and reported.
8. Researcher should have courage in justifying the results.
9. Research should have the guest for knowledge.
10. Research should not be hurried activity.

Why Undertake Research?

Much of our knowledge about sport is based upon research carried out by others. By undertaking systematic investigation into certain areas, we have increased our knowledge about sport dramatically in recent years. The research experts summarise the different purposes of research as follows:

- To investigate some existing situation or problem.
- To provide solutions to a problem.

- To explore and analyse more general issues.
- To construct or create a new procedure or system.
- To explain a new phenomenon.
- To generate new knowledge.

Each of these can be fruitfully applied to many different aspects of sport. A further and equally valid - purpose of research is to allow you to engage with some aspect of sport that interests you, so that you can add to existing knowledge as a personal achievement. Carrying out research into a specific area is one of the best ways to develop our own understanding of a particular area of interest.

DEFINITIONS OF RESEARCH

1. According to Clarke and Clarke

"Research is a careful, systematic and objective investigation, conducted to obtain valid facts, draw conclusions and establish principles regarding an identifiable problem in some field of knowledge".

2. According to John W. Best

"Research is a systematic and objective analysis and regarding of controlled observations that may lead to the development of generalizations, principles, theories and concepts, resulting in prediction, foreseeing and possible ultimate control of events".

3. According to Clifford Woody

"Research is a careful inquiry or examination in seeking facts or principles, a diligent investigation to ascertain something".

4. According to Mouley

"Actually, research is simply the process of arriving at dependable solutions to problems, through the planned and systematic collection, analysis and interpretation of data".

5. According to W.S.Monroe

"Research is the method of studying problems whose solutions are to be derived partly or wholly from the facts".

6. Research is a gradual, continuous and systematically planned scientific method of process.

2

Need and Importance of Research in Physical Education and Sports

The purpose of research is to unfold truth by systematic methods. It may involve the manipulation of concepts or symbols in order to correct or verify the existing knowledge or ideas so that an operational generalization may be made in the shape of a theory.

Physical education is not merely studying human body and its segments, but it is supposed to be the study of the body, mind and soul, in which one cannot be separated from the other. Thus, it is essential to study mind and soul to reveal all the functions of human body. That is why, the inter-disciplinary approach or research with other areas like psychology, sociology, human pathology, physical fitness, sports medicine, exercise therapy, adapted physical education etc. has given new dimensions to the principles and practices in physical education and sports. Without research there is no salvation for the profession of physical education.

Research gives new dimensions to physical education and sports. Physical education started as part of the military preparation in ancient Rome and has now developed into a distinguished discipline. It is needed for the progress of the field of physical Education. If you look at the world records established over the years in track & field, it has stretched the physiological limits of humans only because of the immense research done in the field of human performance.

Research is needed for professional betterment and all round progress. It helps for the invention of new methods, techniques and procedures. E.g., the fosbury style in the high jump was invented by Dr. Dick Fosbury and was implemented in the 1968 Mexico Olympics and soon the athletes realized the biomechanical advantage that they get and currently all the high jumpers in the world use the flop style at the elite level.

Research is needed for the development of new equipments and facilities. E.g., the new swimming suit developed by the speedo company for the Australian swimmers was with a material similar to that of the sharks skin thus reducing the friction in water and a couple of world records were set by the star aussie swimmier Ian Thorpe in the Sydney Olympics.

Research gives pride, prestige, respect, status, and confidence to the physical educationists. It helps to dispel myths about many practices in physical education. Earlier practice of knee rotation has been banned since research proved it would lead to knock-knees. It is useful for the development of scholarly knowledge.

Research helps to solve the critical problems. Participation of women in aggressive sports like boxing has been finally accepted thanks to the research done on participation of women in sports.

Moreover, it helps to prevent Athletic Injuries. The high tech shoes manufactured by companies like adidas reduce the chances of injury.

NEED AND IMPORTANCE OF RESEARCH IN PHYSICAL EDUCATION

Need for research may assume the following factors: -

1. To develop further research

2. To facilitate environmental conditions,

That is through research we find the need to facilitate proper equipments and sophisticated laboratory facilities.

3. To bring professional competency,

That is the development and dissemination of scholarly knowledge is impossible without research.

4. To find new generalization with old data,

Almost every day new performance, new records are being created in sports and games not because human potential has suddenly increased but because principles of various advanced training methods are being extended in the training programmes.

5. Research economies effort and increases efficiency

Research economies all human effort by employing utility of videos, audios, overhead projectors, slide projectors, and LCD projectors for the teachers.

6. Research brings confidence to the teachers

7. Research needs to adapt physical education for physically handicapped children.

The disabled children enjoy and need participation in the games and sports and physical activities.

8. Research leads to the development of appropriate curriculum -

To make the curriculum design effective for different age, sex and standard in the field of physical education and sports.

9. To improve the methods of teaching -

As a result of research, new methods of teaching and coaching are being introduced.

10. Research is necessary to bring a sense of awareness to the teacher of an active research programme.

11. To develop better thinking -

The quality of the research has been improved only through deep thinking. Thus, the term research is highly essential to the physical educationist to think critically and analytically.

12. To explore new training schedules and methods -

Without research there is no exploration and verification in the field of physical education and sports.

13. Research increase prediction -

Physical education research aims at the developing predictions in all facets of education.

14. With the progress of research, the tools and techniques of analysis become modernized and up to date.

The Nature of Research in Physical Education

The object of research is to determine how things are as compared to how they might be. To achieve this, research implies a careful and systematic means of solving problems and involves five characteristics. (Tuckman, 1978).

1. Systematic:- Problem solving is accomplished through the identification and labeling of variables and is followed by the design of research that tests the relationships among these variables. Data are then collected that, when related to the variables, allow for the evaluation of to the variables, allow for the evaluation of the problem and hypotheses.

2. Logical: - Examination of the procedures used in the research process allows researchers to evaluate the conclusions drawn.

3. Empirical: - The researcher collects data on which to base decisions.

4. Reductive: - Research takes individual events (data) and uses them to establish general relationships.

5. Replicable: - The research process is recorded, enabling others to test the findings by repeating the research or to build future research on previous results.

3

Scope of Research in Physical Education and Sports

Research in one sense is wider in its scope more than any other discipline. Thus, the term scope of research in physical education and sports is wide spread throughout the world and has no end.

The scope of research in physical education and sports may assume the following factors:

1. Physical Education as an Academic Discipline

Previously physical education was treated as an extra curricular activity. Now the scope of physical education is treated on a part with other discipline like other History, Economics, Botany and zoology etc.

2. Physical education and professional preparation

Previously, there was no full pledged physical education course available. But now a days the physical education heads and experts in our field are trying to develop our curriculum in such a way so that we are getting C.P.Ed., B.P.Ed., M.P.Ed., M.Phil., B.Sc. Physical Education and also Ph.D., studies

3. Physical Education and Other Sciences

Upcoming sports sciences like Exercise Physiology, Biomechanics, Kinesiology, Sports Medicine, Sports Psychology, Anatomy and Physiology, etc., which contribute substantially to making physical education a unique subject.

4. Research Committee and Councils

A number of research committees have been setup in physical education scientists in various places in the world and they are conducting many researches in the field of physical education and sports. Now a days so many Research publication are excited in the world such as Research Quarterly, Olympic Reviews, Indian

Journals, Sports Psychology research studies, etc., the number of research articles are published in the journals.

5. Human Efficiency and Performance

The research in physical education it improves the efficient work of the physical educationist. By the results of the research the sports performance are improving day to day.

6. Research Laboratory and Doctoral Studies

Now physical education and sports are well established and comprehensive research laboratories such as Sports Exercise, Physiology Lab, Sports Psychology lab, Sports Physiotherapy and Medicine lab, Sports Kinesiology and Biomechanics lab etc., have been setup throughout the world.

7. Role of Physical Education and Natural and Social Sciences

Research strategies in physical education and sports, therefore, derive their strength from those used in natural as well as social sciences in order to scope with problems, of diversified nature such as health, fitness, performance, recreation, learning, teaching - management values etc.

8. Research Publication

Previously there were no research reference books, reviews, and related literature in our field to find out evidences for present studies. But now as day's monthly journals, Research quarterly, half yearly or year magazines are readily available in the market.

9. Consultant and Reconditioning Causalities

Physically educated persons have acted as consultant in the physiotherapy field, as a sports trainers, as a fitness consultant as yoga instructors, etc. They were also engaged by the armed forces, medical services in the physical reconditioning of battle causalities.

10. Dimensions on Conference and Seminars

Now throughout the world there are a number of conferences, seminars, clinics, workshop, and refresher courses to develop the profession and quest for the further research.

11. Research Assistance and Fellowships

Previously there was no fellowship and scholarships to pursue a study in physical education. Now physical education researchers are getting funds, scholarships fellowships on par with other disciplines.

The terms research methods and research methodology are very often confused as one and the same by many researchers. Strictly speaking, they are not the same but show marked differences between them. Basically, research methods are the modus operandi or specific ways of conducting research into a particular subject or topic; they are discrete aspects of research. They are the means, the instruments or the tools the investigator chooses to gather information required to answer his research question. Research methodology, on the other hand, is the "rationale and philosophical assumptions underlying a particular study rather than a collection of methods, though methodology leads to and informs the methods," (Wisker, 2008). It explains the methods by which the researcher may proceed with their research. It refers to the collection of methods the researcher uses in a particular piece of research. That way, research methodology is the science of methods.

More critical is the technical difference between the two terms. Conduct of experiments, tests, surveys, interviews, etc., is straight away related to research methods, whereas research methodology involves acquisition of different techniques or strategies that are considered useful to conduct tests, experiments, surveys and critical studies. The researcher can decode for himself, which technique(s) would suit his research study the best. Some people are better at one kind of research than another. Some people are more interested in one form of question than another. Those are perfectly sound reasons for methodological preferences, but no argument for superiority.

In comparative analysis, research methods refers to the methods or techniques researchers use in performing research operations. They enable researchers to find solutions to research problems, whereas the research methodology aims at the employment of correct procedures to find the solutions. Research methodology may be understood as a science studying how research is done scientifically. It paves the way for the research methods to be employed efficiently and intelligently with no hassle. In it we study the various steps that are generally adopted by the researcher in studying his research problem along with the logic behind them. On this issue, Grix (2004) says:

A project's methodology.......is concerned with the discussion of how a particular piece of research should be undertaken and so can be best understood as the critical study of research methods and their use.

The term refers to the choice of research strategy taken by a particular scholar as opposed to alternative research strategies.

The methodology section should, precisely, not only propose the strategy for answering the particular research question or hypothesis but also a detailed account of all the different methods that would be used to gather requisite data and information. In simpler terms, methodology is the strategy or the approach adopted by a researcher to solve his research problem. While research methodology is the beginning, research methods are the end of any scientific or non-scientific research.

Suppose a scientific research study is to be undertaken to evaluate how aerobic dance training improves cardiovascular endurance of female adolescents, the research methodology will include a thorough understanding of the aerobic exercise techniques - their intensity, training duration to produce desired effects, exercise schedule, etc. as well as the principles of the tests of cardiovascular endurance that are to be employed in order to get the best results from the experiments that are to be performed. Research methods for the same, will include the proper analysis of the results obtained from the experiments conducted by the researcher, and their comparison with the results of similar experiments that have been performed in the past. To gain success the researcher has to have excellence in both the research methods as well as research methodology.

4

Classification of Research

As a process, research may mean to us two things: (1) just the way we do things, and (2) the serious academic activity. For many of us, research refers to accomplishing things such as exploring possibilities for best buys in cars and appliances; going through reviews before book shopping; finding the best schools for our children and ourselves; performing some exercise on career choice. Our search for gathering right kind of information may lead us to interaction with our friends or other knowledgeable people; read articles in magazines, journals, or newspapers; listen to the radio; using libraries, and even exploring the Internet and World Wide Web to obtain information we require for specific purposes. This way, research can be a way of life; it is the basis for taking important decisions in our lives. Without it, we may find it difficult to make a sense of the world around us. This informal, experiential research helps us sift and decipher the flood of information we encounter daily through advertisers, and electronic media.

Formal academic research differs from experiential research; it is highly investigative. For example, it may require us to learn about an area where we have little knowledge or inclination to learn. It may be library-oriented or field-oriented, depending on the nature of the research. Like the everyday research, the academic research is associated with curiosity and intellectual discovery. It is very demanding and challenging in terms of methodological procedures and disciplinary norms and standards. Although many of the concepts and processes of research are generic, academic research is discipline-specific and demands a more rigorous methodology.

As there are several ways of defining research, so there are several traditions of how research can possibly be carried out, distinguished clearly by intentionality on researchers' part. In any field of knowledge, depending upon its nature and purpose, research has three perspectives: the Basic or Fundamental

Perspective, the Applied Perspective, and the Action Perspective This categorization of research perspective is not governed by any hard and fast criteria or rigid rules but by the underlying purposes of the studies undertaken. The findings of a study that may help expand the universe of knowledge and fall under the fundamental research perspective, could also be applied in certain specific situation(s) to solve some problem(s) and they could be of some immediate value to the researcher depending upon the scope and dimensions of the study, sophistication in design and instrumentation involved, and precision of the research findings.

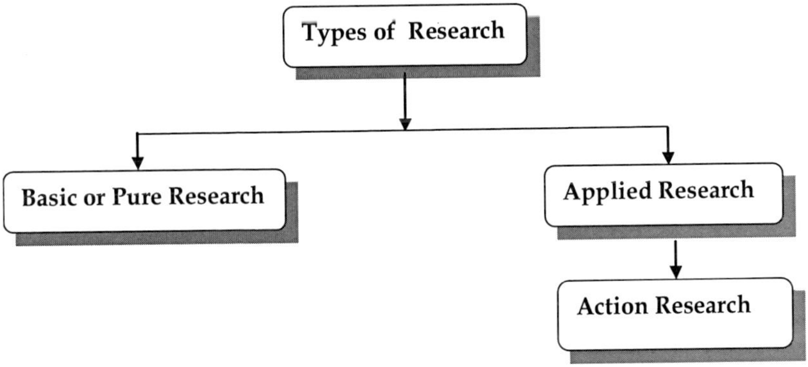

Fig. 1: Scientific research is primarily categorized as basic and applied research

FUNDAMENTAL RESEARCH

Basic (aka fundamental or pure) research is driven by a scientist's curiosity or interest in a scientific question. The main motivation is to expand man's knowledge , not to create or invent something. There is no obvious commercial value to the discoveries that result from basic research. Most scientists believe that a basic, fundamental understanding of all branches of science is needed in order for progress to take place. In other words, basic research lays down the foundation for the applied science that follows.

It is also called as pure research; actually the fundamental or basic research seeks no immediate practical outcome. It seeks to help for the betterment of human life. It seeks to help for the betterment of human life. This research is connected with finding out the universally applicable theories.

"Basic research is designed to add to an organized body of scientific knowledge and does not necessarily produce results of immediate practical value".

For example: - Growth and development, learning theories, heredity and environment, educational values, curriculum etc. The fundamental research is usually carried on in a laboratory situation, some times with the animals as subjects.

Fundamental research can take shape in two ways they are as follows.

1. Discovery of new
2. Development of existing theory.

The best examples of fundamental research are: Robert Boyle's Law (at a fixed temperature, the volume of gas is inversely proportional to the pressure exerted by the gas); Jacques Alexandre Caesar Charles' Law (the density of an ideal gas at constant pressure varies inversely with the temperature); Archimedes' Principle (a body immersed in a fluid is buoyed up by a force equal to the weight of the displaced fluid); Robert Hooke's Law (the relationship between the forces applied to a spring and its elasticity); and Isaac Newton's Laws of Motion.

Basic research is a direct descendent of philosophy, where philosophers and scientists try to grasp the underlying principles of existence. Whilst offering no direct benefits, pure research often has indirect benefits, which can contribute greatly to broadening man's vision about the universe. For example, pure research into the structure of the atom has led to x-rays, nuclear power and silicon chips.

APPLIED RESEARCH

Also called field research in some quarters, applied research is a utilitarian research perspective. Its genesis lies in the basic research, and its primary concern is establishing relationships and testing theories in a field of knowledge for solving specific problems in a practical way, besides attempting to expand the knowledge-base in a domain of knowledge. The applicative value of applied research is immense for this kind of research generally deals with a second level of organization of knowledge, closing the gap between existing basic knowledge and specific practical need in application without attempting to secure complete knowledge beyond the scope of practical application (need). The findings from the applied research are often evaluated in terms of their universal as well as local application. Establishing policy programmes that help to improve social life is the general objective of applied research investigations. Its typical examples are action research, cost-benefit analysis and evaluation research. Applied research may or may not result in inventions or discoveries of much significance, and its findings may or may not be widely generalizable. The greatest volume of research in the science tradition is categorizeable as applied research.

The distinction between fundamental research and applied research is often not very clear for it is not governed by any hard and fast criteria. Scientists who conduct basic research are often influenced by practical issues in determining which topic to study. Precisely, basic research provides fundamental underlying principles that can be used to address specific questions and applied research puts up ideas for the kind of topics that basic research can take up for investigation.

COMPARISON BETWEEN FUNDAMENTAL AND APPLIED RESEARCH

Fundamental Research		*Applied Research*
(1) It's purpose is to develop an appropriate educational theory and to obtain universally applicable principle.	(1)	The Theories developed and the principles derived by the fundamental research are applied in local settings.
(2) Expert training is needed in measurement, research methodology and statistices.	(2)	Simple training and experience is sufficient.
(3) A wide range of methods and comprehensive process is used to locate the problem.	(3)	The range of methods is limited and the process also will not be so comprehensive.

(Contd. ...)

Fundamental Research	Applied Research
(4) An investigator may not be personally involved in the problem he has selected.	(4) An investigator is personally involved in the research problem.
(5) Highly specified and well stated hypothesis are formulated and adopted.	(5) The hypothesis formulated and adopted are not so specific.
(6) It requires a thorough knowledge in the area.	(6) General understanding of the area is sufficient.
(7) A random or unbiased sample of the population is studied. The size of the sample is large and the selection of sample is also quite difficult.	(7) The sample size is small and selection of sample is not so difficult. But the sample should be selected by systematic approach.
(8) A careful attention is neccessary in collecting as well as analysing the data.	(8) Simple procedure will be adopted in collecting and analysing the data.
(9) It is related in solving the problems of day-today life.	(9) It is a professional research.
(10) Much time and efforts are essential in finding the results.	(10) With moderate time and efforts, we can arrive at the results.
(11) Generalisation is possible	(11) Generalisation depends upon the problem.
(12) Findings are usually remain confine to research reports and publications.	(12) The findings are applied in local settings.

ACTION RESEARCH

The action research is the simplest form of applied research and is designed to solve problems that have direct bearing on the context in which research is conducted. It is a systematic investigation through practical action calculated to devise or test new information, ideas, forms or procedures and to produce communicable knowledge. Simplicity, informality and directness are its core characteristics. Carr & Kemmis (1986) considered action research to be "a form of self-reflective enquiry undertaken by participants in social situations in order to improve the rationality and justice of their own practices, and the situations in which these practices are carried out." In it, neither the design, nor the procedures nor the instrumentation, in any way, are sophisticated. There is no control of the extraneous variables. Measurements too are informal and as a result its internal and external validity is poor. Often tailored questionnaires, check lists, and schedules are used to survey situations and collect data. Conclusions are not meant to be generalized. This kind of research has direct relevance to the setting in which it is conducted by "smart" individuals in professions like medicine, teaching or business with an intention to change conditions in a particular situation in which they are personally involved. A primary school physical educator trying to solve certain problem pertaining to skill retention in young children shall be engaging in action research. By all stretch of imagination, action research is less elaborate in procedures and more restricted in applicability. It helps to enhance the competency of the researcher in a particular setting.

RESEARCH PERSPECTIVE – FURTHER CATEGORIZATIONS

There is a different way of categorizing research perspective. In a study the researcher may like to look back and wish to interpret a past situation differently; another research scholar may like to survey the current situations and trends, and a third one may be interested in knowing what effects can be produced when causes are altered under certain circumstances. The first case belongs to historical research or analytical domain, the second descriptive research and the third experimental research.

DESCRIPTIVE RESEARCH

Descriptive research refers to what is currently happening; it attempts to describe (explain in a limited way), within its limits and limitations, why something is happening the way it is happening. Its main purpose is to delineate or depict qualities, characteristics, abilities, behaviours, or opinions of the subjects or quantitative values, the status of a group, an institution, structure or other facilities or to depict trends, fashions or changing values in the society. "A descriptive study (such as survey)," says Best (1983), "describes and interprets what is. It is concerned with conditions or relationships that exist, opinions that are held, processes that are going on, effects that are evident, and trends that are emerging". Research studies conducted in social sciences and business field, where facts are described as they come by, are usually termed as post facto research studies, as opposed to experimental studies.

Generally all kinds of surveys - comparative, retrospective, analytical, evaluative, descriptive, clinical, exploratory, longitudinal, cross-sectional, observational, public opinion, etc. - and case studies (and sometimes philosophical studies also) fall under the ambit of descriptive research. No variable is manipulated in descriptive research nor any variable controlled. Researchers, however, attempt to discover causes of the existing state of affairs without changing the conditions in which things are happening. Descriptive research blends qualitative and quantitative techniques to get at the heart of the problem and reveal truth.

ANALYTICAL RESEARCH

Analysis is detailed examination of some situation or phenomenon with a view to interpret or explain it. Hence, analytical research is an aspect of descriptive research in which the researcher makes a critical evaluation of the already available data for the purpose of arriving at certain valid conclusions in terms of preselected criteria. This kind of research is an eye-opener to the society and the powers-that-be for it sifts the grains of truth from the falsehood of chaff by making an anatomy of the facts deduced.

CONCEPTUAL RESEARCH

Conceptual research is another name for philosophical research. It is non-experimental and is based on logical thinking. It is a systematic and disciplined way of examining abstract ideas, beliefs, values, values systems, standards of life, theories, etc. This is done to develop new concepts about things in various domains of life especially knowledge such as psychology, education, philosophy, religion, etc.

EMPIRICAL RESEARCH

Juxtaposed with conceptual research is empirical or data-based research (i.e. experimental research), whose major supports are observation and experience. Experimental research is deigned to determine casual relationships among variables. The determination cause-and-effect relationships demands that variables, treatments, subjects and conditions be put under strict controls or accounted for throughout the experimentation. The empirical approach is intended to deal with dynamics, forces and interactions. Empirical researchers attempt such kind of studies when they are confident that certain variables (conditions, forces, or factors) influence other variable(s) in some way. Empirical research, without any iota of doubt, is very objective, procedure-based and is an effort towards scoping hard data that serves as a powerful support for a hypothesis under investigation. Empirical method is said to be the brainchild of Aristotle

QUALITATIVE RESEARCH

Qualitative research is concerned with the qualitative aspect(s) of the phenomenon. It is often used in behavioural (social) sciences - psychology, sociology, anthropology, education, etc. - where the chief objective is to discover and understand the motives of human behaviour in various contexts. It involves field work and the qualitative studies yield data in qualitative form as the researcher physically goes to the people setting, site, or institution to observe or record behaviour in its natural setting. Qualitative research is descriptive in that the researcher is interested in process, meaning and understanding gained through words or pictures. By and large, qualitative research is guided by explicit rules and there is great latitude for creative modification and response to the demands of the study. The qualitative researcher is the primary instrument for data collection and analysis. Data are mediated through this human instrument, rather than through inventories, questionnaires, or machines. The physical volume of data is great, often requiring complex systems of organization, data reduction, data display, summarization and translation from specific details to more general expressions. The process of qualitative research is inductive in that the researcher builds abstractions, concepts, hypotheses, and theories from details. Understanding human assumptions, perceptions, beliefs, motives, likes, dislikes, preferences, attitudes, aptitudes, etc., though extremely valuable for many reasons is an uphill task for the data derived from such studies is largely qualitative and is difficult to quantify especially when it is scooped through interviews, projective techniques, opinions, etc. Locke (1989) considers qualitative research to be 'an inferior strategy for discovering cause and effect relationships, accumulating demographic data, determining how much or how may of anything, or providing the basis for generalizing safely from a sample to a population.' According to Meriam (1988), qualitative researchers are concerned primarily with process, rather than outcomes or products. They are interested in meaning.

QUANTITATIVE RESEARCH

The basis of quantitative research is measurement of characteristics, qualities, kinds, traits, etc., of phenomena, things, objects, variables (both concrete and abstract) and humans in quantitative terms. This kind of research is applicable to such events, occurrences, or phenomena as can be expressed in quantity. Hence, quantitative researcher would always be interested in characteristics and actions that are measurable concretely. He attempts to find out meanings which people give to the traits, qualities, characteristics and actions. Guidelines and procedures of quantitative research are rigid as compared to those for qualitative research. Quantified data are easier to treat statistically, making it possible for the researcher to give value judgements while testing a hypothesis. Data quantification is a method of describing observations of materials or characteristics when a defined portion of the material or characteristics is used as a standard for measuring any sample, a valid and precise method of data description is provided. Anthropometric measurements, physiological assessments, market rates, business trends, material and demographic surveys, etc., yield quantitative data. Despite high perceived objectivity, quantitative measurements and the data they yield pose variety of problems such as data ambiguities and inconsistencies are expressed in numerical terms and are thus magnified beyond measure. Saying one out of four students failed in the English test sound far reasonable than saying twenty five percent students failed.

EXPERIMENTAL RESEARCH

All research is scientific because it is systematic and procedure-based, but all scientific research is not necessarily experimental involving interplay of causes and effects and relationships among them. Scientists design experiments or resort to experimental research to determine influences - both quantitative and qualitative - on given phenomena or to determine influences between or among variables of interest. Experimental research is the only research which is considered very objective, realistic, precise and accurate because its designs underscore "controlled observation" of the phenomenon under investigation. Experimentation is a systematic procedure associated with the testing of a hypothesis under known conditions where (a) maximally possible variables are eliminated; (b) careful and critical observation is effected in controlled settings; and (c) by means of a comparative analysis, involving experimental and contrast (control) sampling unites, evidence is sought to establish the presence or non-presence of causation factor for the phenomenon representing the pre-supposed effect. Scientists consider the experimental research as the "most sophisticated, exacting and powerful method for discovering and developing an organized body of knowledge." In experimental studies, variables are manipulated with a view to determining and appraising the effect of their operation on the group(s) involved in the experiment.

Experimental research is categorized into Field Experimentation or Field Study (which may often be longitudinal and observational) and Laboratory Experimentation. In natural field experimentation, no manoeuvring (of conditions, processes and procedures) is needed; in laboratory research conditions are created and studied with utmost precision, control and exactness. Replicability is the hallmark of laboratory research, and artificiality its limitation. How athletes react to the competitive stress during the athletic contests will constitute a field experimentation and how athletes psychologically or physiologically react to training (or exercise) load under controlled laboratory conditions will be an example of laboratory experimentation.

Common Sources of Error in Experimental Research:

Experimental Research attempts to establish cause and - effect relationships. All the types of designs have strength and weakness that pose threat to the validity of research. There are threats to both internal and external validity. Some of the common sources of error or threats to validity are:

Hawthorne Effect

This source of error is named for a research study that was conducted at the Hawthorne electrical plant in the 1920's. It was observed that having a group of workers participate in a research study caused them to feel special so they acted differently than the typical worker. The research study was conducted to determine how changes in the working environment would affect productivity. Results of the study showed that productivity increased no matter whether the change in the working environment was supposed to increase or decrease productivity. This points out that subjects in an experiment may perform in atypical manner due to the newness or novelty of the treatment and because they realize that they are participating in an experiment. This suggests that, as much as possible, the subjects should be unaware that they are participating in an experiment and of the possible outcome of the study.

"John Henry" effect:

In studies with an experimental and a control group, the control group knows it is not supposed to be better than the experimental, and so it tries harder and outperforms the experimental group. This might be called the "Avis effect" after avis cars we are number two, but we try harder. There could be a reverse "John Henry" effect, where the control group gives up.

Rating effect:

Rating effect is usually experienced in studies where subjective ratings are used. It is the commonly observed tendency for a rater to allow previous impressions or knowledge about a certain individual to influence ratings on individual's behaviors. For example, knowing that an individual excels in one or more activities, a judge may rate that person highly on all other activities.

Bias effect:

There are two types of bias that will influence the validity of the experiment,

*Selection bias

*Observer bias error - in rating studies.

Selection bias:

Selection bias occurs when groups are formed on some basis other than random assignment. The differences in performance due to initial selection bias might influence the results of the study.

Observer bias error:

In studies with judges rating the rater might be influenced by his own characteristics and prejudices. While rating a player, racial, sexual and philosophical sources of rating errors may occur.

Ways of controlling threats to validity:

Threats to internal and external Validity are controlled in different ways by specific techniques. One important method is conducting placebo research.

The following are variations of placebo group.

1. Placebo
2. Blind placebo
3. Double blind placebo.

Placebo:

Method of controlling a threat to internal validity in which a control group receives a "false" treatment while the experimental group receives the real treatment.

Blind set-up:

Method of controlling threat to internal validity in which the subject does not know if he or she is receiving the experimental or control treatment.

Double Blind Set-up:

Method of controlling a threat to internal validity in which neither the subject nor the experimenter knows, which treatment the subjects are receiving.

OBSERVATIONAL RESEARCH

Observational research is another name for field or natural study of such phenomena as an epidemic, plant growth, kid's play, crowd behaviour during demonstrations or festivals, etc. In all these cases, no actual condition is disturbed or modified. Situations remain completely natural. An objective and accurate observation is very helpful in understanding phenomena which are difficult to experiment with. Most behavioural studies conducted in sociology and psychology including education are of observational nature. The study of astronomical bodies and their movements, astrological influences on human behaviour are of observational nature. The process of observation becomes more accurate if more sophisticate instruments like computers, high resolution digital and video cameras, telescopes, microscopes, etc., are used to generate requisite data.

In literature, mention is also made of some more research traditions, each one specific to the context and the purpose for which it is undertaken.

- Opinion Research: It is directed at obtaining information calculated to provide grounds for decision or action. Limited in scope, it is highly situation-specific i.e. valid only in the circumstances of the situation enquired into. Properly conducted, it generates enough amount of knowledge. Much market and business research falls into this category. Very little of opinion research is ever published. Conservative scientists are greatly suspicious of it.
- Longitudinal Research: Longitudinal research is a broad term, in which: (1) data are collected for two more distinct periods (implying the notion of repeated measurements); (2) the subjects or cases are the same, or at least, comparable, from one period to the next period.
- Classification Research: It aims at categorization of units into groups; demonstrates differences, and ; explains relationships.
- Comparative Research: The objective of this research is to identify similarities and differences between units at all levels.
- Exploratory Research: It aims at obtaining information about an issue in hand and is used as preliminary reports before a major research study.
- Explanatory Research: Its aim is to explain social relations and events. Researchers use it to build, test or revise a theory.
- Casual Research: It explores the effect of one thing on another and more especially, the effect of one variable on another. The research is used to measure what impact of specific charge will have on existing norms and allows market researchers to predict the hypothetical.

5

Research Problem, Meaning of the Term, Location and Criteria of Selection of Problem, Formulation of a Research Problem, Limitations and Delimitations

A problem in research is infact a gap in the knowledge a situation which requires solution. It is the first step for the discovery of new facts by following certain research procedures.

According to dictionary meaning, problem is a matter, difficult for settlement or solution, a question or puzzle propounded for solution. Human life poses variety of problems.

Research Problem is a matter difficult for settlement or solution, a question or puzzle propounded for solution."

The problem is a question. A felt need, an issue, which needs to be resolved, a difficulty.

It is the first-step for the discovery of new facts by following certain research procedures. Problems are infinite but it is very difficult to locate them for investigation. The selection of a good research problem is considered as a discovery in itself.

LOCATION AND CRITERIA OF SELECTION OF PROBLEM

Locating the problem is the most difficult, but an important phase in research process. Some times, locating a problem itself will be a big problem in research. We can say that locating the problem is a skilful art. It is nothing but the discovery of the problem.

In the discovery of his problem, a researcher has to pass through following procedures. This procedure can save him from wild research and aimless wandering.

(1) Locating a problem area from the broad field of physical education and sports through the survey of related literature.

(2) Selecting problem or printed issue by the process of logical analysis.

(3) Defining and delimiting problems by identifying the variables involved.

(4) Evaluating the research problem.

PRECAUTIONS TO BE FOLLOWED BY A RESEARCHER WHILE SELECTING A PROBLEM

(1) He should select his field of specialisation and become a scholar in that field as early as possible.

(2) He should have a deep interest in it.

(3) Investigator should study critically the available related literature of the problem.

(4) He should accept the difficulties or obstacles of that field as a challenge and try to exercise his originality and ability to tackle them.

(5) He should prepare a record of the problems already studied by others in his area of specialisation.

(6) He should widely discuss any problem that comes to his mind.

THE SOURCES OF PROBLEM

The following are the main sources from which we can select a problem.

(1) Record of Previous Literature :— previous research reports, research bulletins, journals of educational research, bibliographies etc., are the main sources of research problem.

(2) Surroundings :— Class rooms, grounds, indoor halls, swimming pools, athletic track etc., also helps in finding or locating the problem.

(3) Inference from the Theory :— The principles or the theories developed by basic research serves as the source for the problem.

(4) Technological and Social Change :— Social changes and the improvement in the technology brings forth the new problems.

(5) Discussions :— Class room discussions, seminars, exchange of ideas with faculty members and friends may stimulate in selecting a problem.

(6) **Questionning attitude** :– Questionning attitude of a researcher helps in selecting a problem.

(7) **Consultations** :– Consultation with experts, research supervisors and guides is much helpful in selecting a problem.

CRITERIA IN SELECTING A GOOD RESEARCH PROBLEM

Before finalising a problem, several conditions and considerations have to be satisfied. They are called as the criteria in selecting a good problem and they are as follows:–

(1) **Novelty** :– It should be original one and should not involve objectionable duplication. The researcher should not select a problem until he is sure that it really a new problem, which has never before been investigated successfully.

(2) **Interesting** :– It should be an interesting one for the researcher, then only a researcher can work better and do justice.

(3) **Significance of the problem** :– A researcher should select a problem which is significant. It should add knowledge and improve the present practices.

(4) **Researchers Competancy** :– The problem should be selected within the intellectual capacity of the researcher.

(5) **Courage and confidence** :– A researcher should be couragious and confident enough in persuing the study, inspite of the difficulties and social hazards that may be involved. He should work aggressively when data are difficult to gather.

(6) **Feasibility** :– The problem selected should be feasible. It should be according to the interest and competency level of the researcher. The researcher should be skilled enough to develop, administer and interpret the necessary data gathering devices and procedures.

(7) **Availability of data** :– Availability of data is another important factor. The researcher should ensure about the availability of the data for his problem. He should select the sample or subjects in such a way.

(8) **Availability of guidance** :– Every research activity needs proper guidance. Hence, researcher should confirm about the availability of qualified guides and he should obtain the approval from them.

(9) **Availability of co-operation** :– Co-operation of the subjects, authorities, institutions and the co-workers is very much essential in proceeding with the research problem.

(10) **Availability of other facilities** :– The researcher should confirm himself about the availability of other facilities such as finance, time, library, equipments, data gathering devices, administrative considerations i.e., gathering information from various departments, travelling printing etc.

(11) **Level of Research** :– The selection of a problem must be according to the level of research that means Master's degree, M. Phil and Ph.D. etc.

(12) **Experience and Creativity** :– Normally, a good research problem originates from the personal experience of the researcher and it should have creativity.

FORMULATION OF A RESEARCH PROBLEM

Once the general topic or problem has been identified, this should then be stated as a clear research problem, that is, taken from just a statement about a problematic situation to a clearly defined researchable problem that identifies the issues you are trying to address.

It is not always easy to formulate the research problem simply and clearly. In some areas of scientific research the investigator might spend years exploring, thinking, and researching before they are clear about what research questions they are seeking to answer. Many topics may prove too wide-ranging to provide a researchable problem. Choosing to study, for instance a social issue such as child poverty, does not in itself provide a researchable problem. The problem is too wide-ranging for one researcher to address. Time and resources would make this unfeasible and the results from such a study would consequently lack depth and focus.

Statement of Research Problem

An adequate statement of the research problem is one of the most important parts of the research. Different researchers are likely to generate a variety of researchable problems from the same situation since there are many research issues that can arise out of a general problem situation. Your research will be able to pursue only one in depth.

For a problem statement to be effective in the planning of applied research it should have the following characteristics.

- The problem reflects felt needs
- The problem is non-hypothetical, ie it must be based on factual evidence
- It should suggest meaningful and testable hypotheses - to avoid answers that are of little or no use to the alleviation of the problem
- The problems should be relevant and manageable

Formulating the research problem allows you to make clear, both to yourself and the reader, what the purpose of your research is. Subsequent elaboration of method should be oriented to providing information to address that problem. The problem statement is therefore a very important device for keeping you on track with your research. It is also one means by which your research will be evaluated - does the research address the problem as stated.

STEPS IN THE FORMULATION OF THE RESEARCH PROBLEM

The following are Steps involved in formulating a research problem:

1. Identify a broad area of interest in your academic / professional field.

2. Dissect the broad area into sub-areas by having a brain storming session with the colleagues.

3. Select the sub-area in which would like to conduct the research through the process of elimination.

4. Reverse the research questions that would like to answer through the study. This can be after formulation of the objectives of can lead to the formulation of the objective.

5. Assess these objectives to ascertain the feasibility of attaining them in the light of time and other issues like finances and human resource expertise.

THE HYPOTHESIS

A Hypothesis is a tentative assumption drawn from knowledge and theory which is used as a guide in the investigation of other facts and theories which are yet unknown. It is a provisional or an intelligent guess which seems to explain the situation under observation. A hypothesis states what a researcher is looking for.

Importance of Hypothesis

Hypothesis has a very important place in the research, even though it occupies a very small space in the body of the thesis. It is almost impossible to the researcher to go ahead without the hypothesis.

The importance of hypothesis is as given below:

1. It provides direction to research. It prevents review of irrelevant literature and the collection of useless and or excess data.

2. It is a guide to the research process.

3. It focuses the research. With the hypothesis, the research will be like a random, and aimless wondering.

4. It places clear and specific goals before the researcher.

5. It serves as a framework for drawing conclusions. It also helps for the proper interpretation of data.

CHARACTERISTICS OF A GOOD HYPOTHESIS

The characteristic of a good hypothesis are as mentioned below :

1. It must be in agreement with observed facts.

2. It should not have any conflict with any law of nature which is known to be true.

3. It should be stated in a scientific and research like language and not a ordinary statement.

4. It should be stated in a simplest possible terms.

5. It should permit the application of deductive reasoning.

6. It should be so designed that its test will provide an answer to the original problem which forms the primary purpose of the investigation.

7. It should be stated in final form, before any attempt at

varification is made.

Forms of Hypothesis

The hypothesis can be stated in various forms as listed below:

1. Null form
2. Prediction form
3. Declarative form
4. Question form

1. NULL FORM OR NULL HYPOTHESIS

It states that there is no significant difference between the variables concerned. For e.g.: There is no significant diffxxxerence between C.P.Ed. and B.P.Ed. Students as regards physical fitness.

2. PREDICTION FORM

It is chosen because it allows the researcher to state the principles when he actually expects from the experiment. This type of hypothesis is more useful in action research.

3. DECLARATIVE FORM

Generally this type of hypothesis states the relationship between the variables. For e.g., : There is a significant difference between C.P.Ed. and B.P.Ed. Students as regards the intelligence.

4. QUESTION FORM

Sometimes the hypothesis may be in the question form. For e.g.: Is there a significant difference between C.P.Ed. and B.P.Ed. Students as regards physicl fitness?

LIMITATIONS AND DELIMITATIONS OF THE PROBLEM

The limitations and delimitations sections of your research proposal describe situations and circumstances that may affect or restrict your methods and analysis of research data.

Limitations are influences that the researcher cannot control. They are the shortcomings, conditions or influences that cannot be controlled by the researcher that place restrictions on your methodology and conclusions. Any limitations that might influence the results should be mentioned.

When considering what limitations there might be in your investigation, be thorough. Consider all of the following:

- your analysis.

- the nature of self-reporting.
- the instruments you utilized.
- the sample.
- time constraints.

In qualitative research certain limitations might mean that the findings cannot be generalized to the larger population. This is especially true when the definition of the population is broad (ex: elderly women)

Delimitations are choices made by the researcher which should be mentioned. They describe the boundaries that you have set for the study. This is the place to explain:

the things that you are not doing (and why you have chosen not to do them).

the literature you will not review (and why not).

the population you are not studying (and why not).

the methodological procedures you will not use (and why you will not use them).

Limit your delimitations to the things that a reader might reasonably expect you to do but that you, for clearly explained reasons, have decided not to do.

Delimitations define the parameters of the investigation. In educational research the delimitations will frequently deal with such items as population/sample, treatment(s), setting, and instrumentation.

Delimitations include the population of a study, variables, statistical analysis and focus of the research. Within the research proposal, the researcher includes explanations for previous theoretical approaches not under review within the literature review. Typically, a researcher selects one methodology for a study and refers to other possible methodological approaches as delimitations. The parameters of the population must also include justification. Setting delimitations and subsequent justifications helps the researcher maintain objectivity in a study. It also helps other researchers reconstruct a study or advance future research on the same topic. Delimitations provide the scope within which researchers conclude findings and determine a study's reliability or external validity.

Limitations are elements of a study that are not under the control of the researcher. Examples of limitations include funding and time constraints that affect methodology. Limitations decrease the validity of a study, but the research results are still applicable if the researcher discloses limitations and the integrity of the study remains.

It is very important to define and elucidate the problem as a whole, and further define all the technical and unusual terms involved in the statement of the problem.

(1) According to **A.M. Moorthy** "It is the process of separation of problem from the complexities or difficulties and needs".

(2) According to **Whitnew**, "To define a problem, means to put a fence around it and separate it by careful distinction from like questions found in related situations of need".

(3) According to **Clarke and Clarke**, "To define a problem means to specify it in detail and with precision. Each question and subordinate questions to be answered, is to be specified".

A researcher must have to limit and delimit his studies, about the factors which are beyond his control. Delimitation is having a much broader area than the limitation. i.e., immediate fence is called as limitation and the broader fence is called as delimitation. For e.g., time and season of the experiment, the physical and mental status of the subjects, condition of the equipments etc. Limitations may also be expressed about instruments, review of related literature, interpretation techniques etc.

In delimiting, a researcher will have to clarify about,

(1) Geographical setting :— e.g., district, state, country, town etc.

(2) The characteristics of samples :— i.e., age, sex, socio-economic status etc.

(3) Nature and number of variables .— The nature and number of variables to be studied or manipulated should be clarified. For e.g., type of institutions, teachers, coaches, ability level, achievement level etc., have to be specified.

Selected References

Cicciarella, Charles F. (1997) *Research in physical education, exercise science and sport : an introduction.* Scottsdale, Arizona; Gorsuch Scarisbrick.

Gladys Scott (Ed.) (1968) *Research Methods in health, physical education, recreation* (2nd Ed.) Washington, D.C., American Association for Health, Physical Education, and Recreation.

Grix, Jonathan (2004) *The foundations of research.* Houndmills, Basingstoke, Hampshire: Palgrave Macmillan, Palgrave Study Skills: 30-32.

Locke, Lawrence F. (1989) Qualitative research as form of scientific inquiry in sport and physical education, *Research Quarterly for Exercise and Sport.* Vol. 60 (1): 1-20.

Popper, K. (2002). *The Logic of Scientific Discovery* (2nd Ed.). London, UK: Routledge.

Rothstein, Ann (1985) *Research design and statistics for physical education.* Englewood Cliffs, N.J.; Prentice Hall.

Vastrad, Basavaraj, *Methodology of Research in Physical Education and Sports Sciences,* 2000, Khel Sahitya Kendra, New Delhi.

Kutty, Suresh, Kumar, *Research Methodology,* 2007, Sports Publication, New Delhi.

Kamlesh, M.L., *Methodology of Research in Physical Education and Sports. Fourth Editions,* 2005.

UNIT- 2
Survey of Related Literature

6

Need for Surveying Related Literature

Surveys are primarily descriptive in nature. They involve systematic collection, anbysis interpretation and reporting of relevant facts concerning to an institution, sample or population as a whole.

Survey is an important type of study. It must not be confused with the mere clerical routine of gathering and tabulating figures. It involves a clearly defined problem and definite objectives. It requires an expert and imaginative planning, careful analysis and interpretation of the data gathered, and a logical and skilful reporting of the findings.

The major objective of survey is to describe, compare and evaluate present practice. Various types of surveys are conducted. For e.g. :–

(1) **Descriptive survey** :– Concerned with describing a specific set of phenomina at a point in time.

(2) **Comparative survey** :– Intended to compare two or more research situations in terms of some pre-selected criteria.

(3) **Evaluative survey** :– Planned to evaluate some aspect of research situation in terms of pre-selected criteria.

(4) **Normative** :– It deals with the construction or compilation of norms.

(5) **Informative** :– It provides information about an individual,

or an institution. Almost all the case studies are informative in nature.

TOOLS OF SURVEY STUDIES

Survey study mainly depends upon certain procedures, they are also called as tools of survey studies. They are :—

(1) Observation.

(2) Questionnaire.

(3) Interview.

(4) Opinionnaire.

(1) OBSERVATION

The observation is directed towards the watchful and critical attention with a view of ascertaining to a fact. It is a primary step in the research prediction and interpretation are the important techniques of observation. Observation is the earliest technique used by human being to acquire knowledge both philosophic and scientific.

The mother observes child, the teacher observes the students, the coach observes the players. As a scientific tool of research, observation is multi-dimensional activity aiming to help the researcher to record the accuracy of the events in various ways.

Observation may be longitudinal or cross sectional. Longitudinal observation refers to the study of one phenomenon over a long period of time. For e.g. growth and development of children. Where as cross-sectional observation, a variety of phenomena are observed. For e.g., more than one team are observed simuntaniously in a short duration.

The researcher must precisely know how to observe, what to observe, how to record and what to record. The observation may be recorded,

(1) Manually

(2) Photography

(3) Cinematography

(4) Audio and video recording etc.

The researcher must also be prepared about the following

aspects for the observation :—

(1) Systematisation of observation
(2) Check lists
(3) Schedule
(4) Rating scale
(5) Score card

(2) THE QUESTIONNAIRE

Questionnaire is one of the most extensively used data gathering technique with researchers engaged in descriptive studies. It is a set of questions, logically arranged in sequence and used when functional information is needed. A questionnaire is intended to secure information on the status or current practices of individuals, groups or institutions regarding such matters as health, motivation, status, curriculum facilities etc.

The mailed questionnaire is one of the most used and probably most criticised data-gathering device. It can reach more people over a wide geographical area quickly and at a relatively low cost.

TYPE OF QUESTIONNAIRE

(1) **Structured and non-structured** :— The structured questionnaire contains definite, concrete and directed questions, whereas non-structured may consist of partially completed questions or statements.

(2) **Closed form and open form** :— The questions that requires a very short answer or checks are called as restricted type or closed type. The answers may be yes or no, tick a mark (Ö). This type of questinnaire is easy to furnish the details, takes less time, it is relatively more objective, more acceptable and convenient to both the respondent and the researcher for the tabulation and analysis.

The open end form of thesis, requires a free response in the respondents own words. Sometimes it is difficult to interpret, tabulate and summerise in the research report. Therefore many questionnaires include both type of questions i.e., open end and closed end.

CHARACTERISTICS OF A GOOD QUESTIONNAIRE

Following are the some of the characteristics of a good

questionnaire :—

(1) It deals with an important or significant topic so that it encourages respondent to respond.

(2) It seeks only that data which cannot be obtained from the resources like books, reports and records.

(3) The questions are objective, no hints, clues or suggestions are given.

(4) Leading questions are carefully avoided.

(5) It is as short as possible because long questionnaires are normally threw away in the waste-paper basket.

(6) It is attractive in appearance, neatly arranged and clearly duplicated or printed.

(7) Questions are proceeding from simple to more specific.

(8) Various categories are arranged to get the easy and accurate answers.

(9) Descriptive adjectives and adverbs are avoided. For e.g., words like frequently, rarely, occasionally etc.

(10) Double negatives are avoided.

(11) It is easy to tabulate, summarise and interpret.

(12) Coding is done for the easy use of mechanical tabulation.

CONSTRUCTION OF THE QUESTIONNAIRE

A researcher can not get a ready made questionnaire, suitable for his study. He has to prepare it for himself. He should take great care in developing or constructing a questionnaire that will ansure accurate and valid responses, which will produce meaningful informations. For this a researcher must be thorough in the field to be surveyed.

The following are the some of the suggestions for the construction of a questionnaire :—

(1) The purpose of the survey should be clearly mentioned.

(2) The investigator should out line the field of study - Broad categories of information should be identified, so that overlapping can be avoided and the questions should be developed in an orderly manner.

(3) The questions should be arranged in a logical manner -

questions should proceed from simple to complex.

(4) All the questions must be very clear - the terms used should be defined.

(5) Pictures and diagrams may be used to clarify certain particular situations.

(6) Questions with double meaning or double implication must be avoided.

(7) Double negatives should be avoided.

(8) Leading questions should be avoided.

(9) Short answer type and objective type of questions must be included.

(10) Precoding for the data processing should be considered.

THE INTERVIEW STUDY

Interview is an important tool of research. It is a formal meeting of the investigator and the interviewee. It is an oral questionnaire. Instead of writing the response the interview gives the required information orally and face-to-face.

There are several kinds of interviews varying in scope and objectives :—

(1) Structured interview :— A structured interview involves pre-determined question-schedule and highly standardised recording technique. The procedure is some what rigid.

(2) Unstructured interview :— An unstructured interview is characterised by flexibility and freedom of supplementary questions.

(3) Clinical interview :— It's purpose is to know the feelings, motivations and life experiences which influences human behaviour.

Through the interview technique, the researcher can stimulate the subject to greater insight into his/her own experiences and there by gather significant information which was not anticipated.

If the interviewee is agreeable, a tape recorder should be used for the convenient and effective recording of the interview. It eliminates writing during the interview, which may be distraction for both, the investigator as well as the respondent.

The following are the some of the characteristics of interview: –

(1) It helps in obtaining the confidential information.
(2) The personal contact helps in drawing out the informing by on-the-spot follow-up questions, which is not possible by the mailed questionnaire.
(3) Interpretation of the meaning of questions is possible.
(4) The interview provides an opportunity for the investigator to give information and to develop good relationship with the respondent.

OPINIONNAIRES

Opininnaire is a type of questionnaire which is used to find out what and how people feel about other individuals, institions, events and organisations. The basic purpose of the opinonnaire is to enable the researcher to predict the behaviour of people in a particular set of situations or to anticipate the course of events.

Opinion and attitude are normally used in a more or less synonymous manner, but there is a slight difference between these two. **An opinion** is just an expressed attitude, it may not lead to any type of activity in a particular direction whereas an attitude compels the individuals to act either favourably or unfavourably according to what they perceive to be correct.

An attitude is a tendency of an individual to react in a certain way towards a particular object, stimulus, situation, process or phenomenon. Attitude is what a person feels or believe in. It is the inner feeling of an individual it may be either positive, neutral or negative.

Opinionnaires or attitude scales are used in physical education and sports, specially when it is necessary to know the attitude of students, toward their teachers and coaches, of parents towards physical exercise, of players toward team officials etc. Certainly the success of physical education as a profession depends upon the attitudes, people have about the profession in general. Opinionnaire or attitude scales are a good device of evaluating the existing policies and practices in sports and physical education.

An attitude scale or opinionnaire may be in the form of questionnaire, which carries precise questions, or it may be in the form of a check list or a schedule. A coach or a physical education teacher may directly ask the players how they feel about a match, about the officials or even about himself.

Measurement of opinion is closely related to the real feelings or attitude. Some measures have been devised to measure attitudes, they are as follows :—

(1) Asking the individual directly how he feels about a subject through the use of a schedule, questionnaire or interview.

(2) Asking the individual to check the statements in a list with which he is in agreement.

(3) Asking the individual to indicate the degree of his agreement or disagreement with a series of statements about a controversial subject.

(4) Inferring an individuals attitude from his reaction to projective devices through which he may reveal his attitude unconsciously.

There are many instruments to evaluate the opinionnaire. Two of them have been explained below:—

(1) Likert scale

(2) Q-sort

(1) LIKERT SCALE

Likert scale is a technique employed to indicate percentage responses for each individual statement which represents sentiment of approval or disapproval toward a phenomenon. The stronger the feeling, higher will be the rating, it may move toward reverse - when stronger feelings have negative relations.

In the likert scale, approval or disapproval of a given phenomenon is determined by the degree of subjects agreement or dis-agreement with each statement on a five point scale. Normally a statement will be given and the respondent has to answer or give his opinion according to the degree of feeling, by ticking the appropriate response. The degrees are as follows :—

Degree of response	Scale Value or (Points)
(1) strongly approve or strongly agree	5
(2) Approve or agree	4
(3) Undecided	3

(4) Disapprove or disagree 2

(5) Strongly disapprove or strongly disagree 1

The high scores always reflects the best attitude. Therefore a score of 5 may accompany strongly agree in some cases and strongly disagree in some others.

(2) Q-SORT

It is a technique of scaling the objects or statements, specially when more number of items are given for ranking. The Q-sort is used to asses the attitudes, values, artistic judgements, interests of subject or practices. For e.g., it may be employed to assess what importance should be given to the activities which are suggested for the improvement of physical fitness. In such situations, more numbers of cards or slips should be prepared, and each one should carry the name of different activity such as sports, games, activities to develop strength, speed, agility, endurance etc.

The Q-sort is like a questionnaire, normally having 9 to 11 levels, such as least important to most important or least desirable to most desirable and so on. For e.g.

Least important *Most important*

scale	1	2	3	4	5	6	7	8	9
%age of slips	2	7	13	18	19	17	13	8	3

The numbers listed on the top line are the scale values and the bottom line are the percentage of slips in each scale category.

PROFILES

These studies are done in order to show the various trait patterns. Profiles helps in the placement of the individual on test scales for a number of characteristics. By comparing the capacities on a common scale, individual's strengths and weaknesses can be found out. For the comparison, the norms already constructed may be used or fresh norms may be constructed from the samples of the population to which the subjects belong.

The 'T' scale is a convenient scale for this purpose, although other scales have also been used.

The study conducted by Shelley brings out that although many successful athelets generally have common characteristics, the pattern of these characteristic vary from one athlete to the other. He had given an example of 14 year old high school athlete. His profile showed that he was very good in foot ball, basket ball, and hurdles. He was also playing summer base ball. But according to his age group - he was physically immature and was average on body size. Even then, he was good in speed, agility, muscular power and muscular endurance. His physique was stroghly mesomorphic and was very intelligent.

All these information can be studied from the profile

CASE STUDY

The case study is a complete analysis and report of the status of a particular individual, subject, school, institutions, playgrounds or community with a view to ensure the possible improvement. The aim of case study is to understand the life-cycle of an important part of the life cycle of an individual, an institution or a social group or community. The case study is a diagnostic study. The case study of individuals may be done on great scientists, artists, outstanding sports persons etc.

CHARACTERISTICS OF A GOOD CASE STUDY

A good case study should have the below mentioned characteristics :—

(1) It should be based on adequate and complete data.

(2) It's data should be valid.

(3 It should have continuity.

(4) It's records should be kept confidential.

(5) It's data should be scientifically and systematically recorded. And it should be diagnostic one.

(6) It's follow up-work should be undertaken.

ADVANTAGES OF CASE STUDY

The case studies are having the following important advantages :—

(1) It helps the researcher to have a clear picture about the **'case'** directly.

(2) It is an important medium of tracing out the natural history of the social unit under study.

(3) Intensive and extensive study of the case is possible only through this technique.

(4) Case studies help to achieve certain therapeutic and administrative purposes.

(5) This is the best technique in social research to gather and generalise the knowledge.

(6) It also suggests the measures to be taken for the improvement of the unit.

DATA GATHERING IN CASE STUDY

The following procedures are used in collecting the data for case study :—

(1) Psychophysical examination :— Vision, hearing, speech, neuro-muscular co-ordination, etc.

(2) Medical examination :— Height, weight, nutrition general health, diseases etc.

(3) Mental condition :— General intelligence through verbal and non-verbal tests.

(4) Temperamental aspects :— Emotions, complexions interests, attitudes, sentiments and character etc.

(5) Educational history :— Qualification, awards and scholarships, ranking, etc.

(6) Family History :— Ancestory, parents, sublings, home conditions, economic status, relations, attitude of parents toward the society and sports etc.

To collect the information about all these respects, a researcher has to use observation, interview and questionnaires. He has to collect paper cuttings, photos from albums, certificates, school records, court judgements etc.

7

Literature Sources and Library Readings

Libraries play a vital role in the process of research. The scientific research needs a library and laboratories, where as for humanistic research, libraries play the role of laboratories also. Previously libraries were considered as the store house of information, but now-a-days, they are not merely store houses, but their prime duty is to provide the available information, i.e., right information to the right user at the right time.

A researcher visits many libraries to collect information. Hence, he must know what are all the materials available in a library, how to locate them and how to make use of them. Every researcher should have some basic knowledge about the library. Otherwise, he is simply a hunter lost in the forest.

Proficiency in the use of library or in the review of the literature consists of

(1) The ability to locate the sources directly.

(2) The ability to go through the various sources quickly.

(3) The ability to select relevant material.

(4) The ability to organise properly what has been selected and accumulated, and

(5) The ability to interpret the material.

Many libraries provide a printed guide, which includes the diagram indicating the location of racks, periodicals, rooms, reference division, micro film equipment, chippings, computers, floppy's, CD's etc. Of course, the librarians will be there for help, but the researcher should not depend much upon him, he must also be proficient.

NOTE TAKING

Review of related literature demands systematic and simultaneous note-taking during the reading. A researcher is advised to use the "Reference cards" which are normally stiff ruled cards of 4" × 6" or 5" × 8". They are also called as "Index cards".

The reference notes may be classified under four main categories as mentioned below :—

(1) **Quotations** :— The reader reproduces the exact words of the author and copies the material accurately. Exact page number must also be taken down to put on the footnote.

(2) **Paraphrase** :— The author's ideas are restated in the readers own words.

(3) **Summery** :— The reader records the content of the material read by him in a condensed form. It is the shortened list of the vast material.

(4) **Evaluation** :— The reader writes, what the author says, then reacts about it, then indicates his agreement or disagreement with the author.

THE LIBRARY METHOD

Traditionally, a library is a "place in which books, manuscripts, musical scores, or other literary, and artistic materials are kept for use, but not for sale" (Prashar, 2003). The library tradition is, perhaps, one of the oldest literary traditions of the mankind, which must have begun in the hoary past of human civilization. Down the memory lane, some of the most famous libraries of the ancient world included Villa of the Papyri (79 C.E.), the Royal Library of Ashurbanipal (612 B.C.) in Nineveh, Library of Pergamum (197 B.C. -159 B..C., Library of Celsus (135 A.D.) in the city of Ephesus, Imperial Library of Constantinople (330 A.D.), the Royal Library of Alexandria (295 B.C.), Takshasila (6th 5th century B.C.), Nalanda (founded in 427 and considered "one of the first great universities in recorded history, it was sacked by Turkic Muslim invaders under Bakhtiyar Khilji), Academy of Gurdishapur (3rd through 6th century), House of Wisdom (9th-13th century, Baghdad), Nippur Temple Library (2500 B.C.), Ebta (2500 B.C. - 2250 B.C.), the oldest organized yet discovered, etc. Unfortunately, many of these institutions of great learning had been victim to the vandalism of the barbaric expansionist designs and religious fanaticism of the enemies of mankind.

Under the impact of recent electronic boom and computer

science revolution, libraries have undergone an irreversible transformation in structure, form and function. Importantly, library is a social institution entrusted with the sacred responsibility of collecting, organizing, preserving and disseminating knowledge and wisdom using the most modern scientific methods and means without completely severing it ties with the traditionally good. Acquisition, organization, preservation and documentation of information in whatever form it exists, expeditiously, pin-pointedly and exhaustively are the basic features of a library. Unprecedented explosion in information and information technology have made a shift in this paradigm, and accessing and utilization of vast amount of information has become the major concern of libraries.

Libraries, both the traditional and the digital, are a repository of human knowledge and wisdom. Whatever subjects or ideas humans have ever pondered will be found in your academic library. Not only will you find the texts of great thinkers and writers, but you will also find millions of articles and books by scholars who have spent countless hours interpreting and deciphering the vast universe of human knowledge. With substantial growth - both vertical and horizontal - and diversification in objectives, libraries today have come to be "broadly categorized as public libraries, academic libraries, and special libraries to suit different categories of readers" (Prashar, 2003). With the support of modern technology, tremendous transformation has been brought about in the library system and information science. According to Prashar (2003) : "'Library without walls', 'paperless society', 'information support centre', 'disembodiment of libraries', 'world at our finger tips', 'virtual library' and the like denote phases of library-technology relationship." Without libraries, the cultural memory is lost, without cultural memory, society cannot continue to function. What know today is based on the foundations of what was known. We are pygmies standing on the shoulders of the giants.

Irrespective of its physical dimensions, a typical library categorically has a borrowing section, a reference section, a periodical section, a children's section, etc. A detailed diagram at the library entrance provides vivid details about the location of the stacks, room for periodicals, reference division, reading rooms, place for special collection of books, microfilm and micro-card reading equipment, location for clippings, manuscripts, pamphlets, internet facilities, etc. Some other part of the library subscribes the names of special indexes, abstracts or other references available.

Moving with the spirit of time, most public libraries and university libraries have gone digital. A digital library is a computer-based system for acquiring, storing, organizing, searching and distributing digital materials to the user, and access. It is not network based but designed to be capable of being attached to a network. This has made the libraries more user friendly and access to literature as well as search for desired material speedier, economical and focused than ever before. The Library offers a range of training for research students that will assist with the production of literature reviews including sessions on electronic databases, using the bibliographic management software EndNote to download records, Internet searching using Netscape, Library catalogue searching, off-campus student orientation, subject resources, and research skills.

LOCATING REFERENCE MATERIAL

In all standard libraries, the reading material is systematically arranged and securely stored. We can find it with the help of library card catalogues - an alphabetical listing of books. A library catalogue is a comprehensive, organized list of a library's contents: It refers to books, maps, periodical archives, artwork, computer files, microfilm, etc. Though library catalogues are limited to a particular library, nearly all library catalogues today share the same basic search features and organization. Each card carries a library call number, author(s)' name, date of birth of the author(s), name of the publisher, place of publication, year of publication, library classification call number, and the like. After the advent of online catalogues in the '70s, physical card catalogues became nearly obsolete, but some libraries retain their card catalogues for decorative or commemorative purposes. Instead the substantial shift has occurred in favour of computerized card catalogues.

Using a catalogue card, a person should be able to find, identify, select and obtain a book knowing either the author, title, or subject. The catalogue should show the user all books that a library owns by any given author, subject, or type of literature; and that it should be useful in guiding the user's choices regarding a book's edition and character. In 1960s, the Library of Congress created a catalogue format called Machine-Readable Cataloguing (MARC), which allowed for quicker processing of bibliographic records; that development led to Online Public Access Catalogues (OPACs), which were considerably cheaper to maintain than physical catalogues and were so quickly adopted by most libraries.

The aim of literature search primarily is to make an authentic and optimum search for relevant material especially articles or research papers, and exclude the irrelevant i.e. trivial and trash than often gets inserted in the literature review advertently or inadvertently. Another objective is to make the literature search process feasible and economical in terms of time, effort and cost. Notably, a comprehensive literature search adds credibility to the study when a well-balanced viewpoint is put up by recalling and citing divergent studies.

OPTIMIZING LITERATURE SEARCH

In order to optimize literature search, the researcher needs to have a basic understanding of the database, how literature is organized and indexed in a library, how different databases differ from one another, how search engines can be harnessed to obtain relevant information, how search engines are different from databases, and how different search searches can be made. Almost akin to recce (reconnaissance) in military nuances, the searching process enables the researcher to lay his or her hand on the material of their interest. In a good university library, there are more diverse sources of material relevant to research studies than found elsewhere.

While general databases include Index Medicus, Web of Science, EMBASE, CAB, Cochrane, etc., specific databases cover PsychInfo, CANCERLIT, CINAHL, AMED, and CIRRIEork. Apart from these, a physical education researcher may benefit from searching the following selected but important indexes:

(a) Business index no, and index of journals.

(b) Bibliographics and indexes - International Periodical Index, Bibliographies and Summaries in Education; Completed Research in Health, Physical Education & Recreation; Research Completed and Underway in Health, Physical Education & Recreation, Annual Bibliographies of Completed Research in

Health, Physical Education and Recreation; Research in Education.

(c) Indexes of Books - Bibliography Index; Cumulative Boos Index, Doctoral Dissertation, Library Of Congress Catalogue, Publisher's Weekly Index, Government Printing Office Catalogue, Books in Print, Forth Coming Books.

(d) Index of Facts and Statistics - Accident facts, Biennial Survey in Education, Brief Facts, Business Statistics, Statesman's Year Book, Almanac and Year Book.

(e) Reviews and Abstracts - Dissertation Abstracts.

(f) Encyclopaedia of Associations.

(g) Ulrich's International Directory of Periodicals.

In addition, many computerized indexing systems have been installed in most libraries. They include on-line indexes, Info TVac, Internet Resources, etc. In searching indexes, the researcher may have to look under various subject headings other than the title of his topic. Related topics should also be searched in addition to specific ones.

Books are classified and systematically placed in the library, so tracing out the requisite source of material is not difficult if one is familiar with the library book classification systems. The two major systems of classifying books are Dewey Decimal System (used in small libraries) and Library of Congress System (in vogue in large libraries). In ***Dewey Decimal System***, various subjects have been allotted different numbers under 10 major categories running from 000 to 999 with appropriate decimal placing for different classes and subcategories under each subject heading : for example, 100 - Sociology; 300, 310-Statistics; 320-Political Science; 350-Administration; 360-Associations and Institutions; 370-Education; 700-Fine Arts; 800-Literature; 900-History and so on with a provision for an open-ended classification procedure in decimal fractions in each case. ***Library of Congress System*** provides for 20 main classifications instead of 100 as in Dewey decimal system. In this system, the English alphabets from A to Z are used as classification symbols in various combinations : for example, A - General Books; B - Philosophy and Religion; C- Geography and Anthropology; GV - Physical Education & Recreation; H - Sociology; L - Education; LB - Physical Education, Health Education and

Recreation; M - Music; N - Fine Arts; R - Medicine, etc. Familiarizing with the library classification system is necessary so as to economize on his time and energy in locating the material and getting straight away to it.

LITERATURE SEARCH BY INTERNET

Samuel Johnson once said that "a man will turn over a library to make one book." This quote indirectly refers to the difficulty in procuring material for research and writing. Enormous amount of time and money are required for this notwithstanding. The modern computer technology has come to the researcher's rescue by providing them the swiftest means of accessing knowledge - the Internet. By simply moving the cursor and clicking a button, the researcher is taken to vast expanse of the latest knowledge in any subject - art, science, professional practice and/or application, in a twinkle.

Internet is a network of interconnected networks not managed by any one central agency but by several organizations working in cooperation with one another. It is an impressive combination of information and communicative software artefacts, and activity, an object as well as a process. (It is) a global web of computer networks that was made instantaneous ad decentralized global communication possible. From the users' viewpoint, it is a huge warehouse of text, information, audios, videos and animations. The amount of information available through the Internet is staggering. It is the cheapest and the fastest means to (a) get information, (b) provide information, and (c) compute information.

With the help of general search engines like Yahoo, Google, MSN, Meta-searches, and specific search engines such as Google scholar, Scirus, OAI-Harvester, Med-Hunt, etc., it is possible to get at the general databases such as Index Medicus, Web of Science, EMBASE, CAB and Cochrane; and specific databases like PsychINFO (1967-), CANCERLIT, SPORTDiscus (1975-), CINAHL, AMED, Web of Science (1965-) and CIRRIEork. However, Thomas, Nelson & Silverman (2005) caution that "correctness and accuracy of information (received through Internet) is often difficult to verify. In fact, much of it is wrong and misleading." It is, therefore, necessary not to depend too much on this information source.

CRITERIA FOR GOOD NOTE-TAKING

It is highly disappointing when a note which has been taken after a great search and study is found to be not clear enough. Therefore a researcher should beer in mind the below mentioned aspects while note-taking:—

(1) Skim the reference source before taking any notes. A bird's-eye view is essential before one can decide what material to record and use, selecting the most significant material is a skill to be cultivated.

(2) File each note card under a definite topic or heading. A complete bibliographic citation should be made to facilitate the location of the book in future.

(3) Include only one topic on a card. If the matter is lengthy, the consequetive numbered cards should be used and they should be hired before filing.

(4) Be sure that notes are complete, and clearly understandable.

(5) Distinguish clearly between a summery, a direct quotation of the author and an evaluative statement.

(6) Do not plan to recopy or type your notes. It will waste the time and increases the possibility of error and confusion.

(7) Keep some spare note cards always with you, because some times you may get the ideas, while waiting, travelling, or listening to a lecture.

(8) Be careful not to loose your notes. Tie them as soon as they are copied.

(9) Keep a permanent file of your notes, they may be required in a number of occasions.

(10) Transfer the notes to microfilms, floppy's and C.D.Roms, which are very useful.

BIBLIOGRAPHY

As the researcher goes through the related literature, he must prepare the bibliography. Bibliography is nothing but listing down the titles of the books referred with their author's names. For footnoting, the page number also must be recorded. The main purpose of the bibliography is to have it in the proper form as an appendix in the final report. All the books or magazines may not be recorded. Only important books which referred should be recorded. While preparing a bibliography a systematic procedure should be adopted. i.e., if the books are referred, the title of the book, author's name, publishers name and address, number of the edition and year of publication must be noted. If the magazines or other sources (Thesis or dissertations) are referred, then the name of the magazine, number of the volume, month and year, name of the author of that article, and incase of thesis, the title of the topic, name of researcher, if possible to which institution it was submitted and for what purpose it was submitted should be noted.

A well recorded and annotated bibliography will provide a up-to-date material for the next researcher.

Some of the sources of literature that are found in the libraries are listed below :—

(1) Encyclopedias.

(2) Research abstracts, thesis and dissertations.

(3) Bibliographies and directories.

(4) Year books.

(5) Dictionaries.

(6) Reference books.

(7) Research journals and periodicals.

(8) Educational indices.

(9) Surveys and survey report.

(10) Documents.

(11) Hand books. etc.

RESEARCH REVIEWS

In the literature search the research reviews have got very important role in physical education and sports. Many research reviews have been published, some of the reviews have been listed below :—

(1) Contributions of physical activity to human well being.

(2) Fiftieth anniversary issue of research quarterly for exercise and sports.

(3) Physical fitness research digest.

(4) Exercise and sports science reviews.

(5) Science and medicine of exercise and sports.

(6) An encyclopedia of physical education, fitness and sports.

(7) NAGWS - research report.

(8) Exercise and aging, and so many.

THE CARD CATALOG

The card catalog is nothing but an index of all the publications in a particular library. The card catalog will be of three types, as mentioned below :–

(1) The author card.

(2) The subject card.

(3) The title card.

And in all the cards, the call numbers will be given. With the help of these "cards" the researcher can immediately locate the required publications on the book selves.

INDICES

Some times an investigator has to refer the periodicals of several years. For locating the literature from such sources he requires index of particular periodicals. The bibliographic index, educating index, journals in education, psychological index, etc., are called as standard index. And the below mentioned are some of the physical education indexes :–

(1) Research quarterly, Indices

(2) Physical fitness/sports medicines Index.

(3) Physical education Index.

(4) Physical education/sports Index. etc.

ABSTRACTS

Abstracts are very much helpful in searching the relevant literature, and many journals will provide the abstracts. For e.g., volume of completed research in Health, Physical Education and Recreation. Abstracts of eaesrrch papers etc. Abstracts will provide the summery, conclusion and recommendations for the further research. Given below is the list of abstracts of various other fields which are allied with physical education :–

(1) Nutritional abstracts and reviews.

(2 Wistor institute of anatomy & biology abstracts.

(3) Education abstract.

(4) Exceptional child abstracts.

(5) Psycological abstracts etc.

BIBLIOGRAPHIES

Like indices, number of bibliographies are also prepared and made avoidable to the research workers in the field of physical education.

A list of some of the bibliographies is given below: –

(1) American physical education review.

(2) List of doctoral thesis completed from-to-. Some bibliographies were prepared even other than the research reports, they are : –

(i) Branc Robert M. "An annotated and indexed bibliography of Basket Ball - publications 1946.

(ii) Stewart M.W. "An indexed bibliography of selected football references" 1948.

(iii) "Annotated bibliography on movement education "1977.

(iv) "Bibliography of research involving female subjects" 1975.

MICROFICHE REPRODUCTIONS

Micro fiche is an electronic device of 4" × 6"which can reproduce approximately 96 pages of a thesis. Previously it was used for the reproduction of unpublished doctoral thesis and master's dissertation. The microfiche requires a special machine to read, and it is almost outdated now a days, and the floppys and C.D.'s have replaced them. They are most convenient and can produce thousands of pages.

SELECTED PERIODICALS

Given below is the list of some of the periodicals connected and allied to physical education : –

(1) International journal of sports medicine.

(2) International journal of sports psychology.

(3) International review of sports sociology.

(4) Journal of biomachanics.

(5) Journal of educational psychology.

(6) Journal of educational research.
(7) Journal of physical education, recreation and dance.
(8) Journal of sports history.
(9) Journal of sports behaviours.
(10) Journal of sports medicine and physical fitness.

LITERATURE REVIEW

A literature review is an account of what has been published on a topic by accredited scholars and researchers. Some call it a careful examination of a body of literature pointing towards the answer to the research question under focus. All good research studies are guided by a review of the relevant literature. The literature review serves as a mechanism by which your research is viewed as a cumulative process. As a researcher, it gives you the most humbling experiences you are likely to have because in most likelihood you may find out that just about any worthwhile idea you will have has been thought of before, at least to some degree. That is the reason why it becomes an essential part of a thesis or research report and an integral component of the scientific process. Aftabi (1992) rightly points out: "A good literature review requires knowledge of the use of indexes and abstracts, the ability to conduct exhaustive bibliographic searches, ability to organise the collected data meaningfully, describe, critique and relate each source to the subject of the inquiry, and present the organised review logically, and last, but by no means least, to correctly cite all sources mentioned. " The literature review is designed to identify related research, to set the current research project within a conceptual and theoretical context.

Purpose of Literature Review

In writing the literature review, your purpose is to convey to your reader what knowledge and ideas have been established on a topic, and what their strengths and weaknesses are. As a piece of writing, the literature review must be defined by a guiding concept (e.g., your research objective, the problem or issue you are discussing, or your argumentative thesis). Regardless of the research method used, the purpose of the literature review remains the same i.e. to test your research question against what already is known about your subject. According to Bruce (1994): "The review forms an important chapter in a thesis where its purpose is to provide the background to and justification for the research undertaken."

By another viewpoint, the purpose of a review is to analyze critically a segment of a published body of knowledge through summary, classification, and comparison of prior research studies, reviews of literature, and theoretical articles. It is not just a descriptive list of the material available, or a set of summaries, but a critical analysis (evaluation) of how the studies conducted by others acclaim or disclaim the truth of your hypothesis. Through the literature review you will discover whether your research question already has been answered by someone else. If it has, you must change or modify your question.

Dena Taylor of Health Sciences Centre says that a literature review must (a) be organized around and related directly to the research question the researcher is developing; (b) synthesize results into a summary of what is and is not known; (c) identify areas of controversy in the literature; and (d) formulate questions that need further research. Bruce (1994) has identified six elements of a literature review: a search, a survey, a comparison, a vehicle for learning, a research facilitator, and a report. Besides enlarging your knowledge about the topic, writing a literature review lets you gain and demonstrate skills in two areas: (1) *Information seeking*: the ability to scan the literature efficiently, using manual or computerized methods, to identify a set of useful articles and books; and (2) *Critical appraisal*: the ability to apply principles of analysis to identify unbiased and valid studies.

The ***role of literature review*** in a research study is critical for several reasons- both implicit and explicit.

- Literature review *exposes the main gaps in knowledge* and identifies major areas of dispute and uncertainty. Becoming aware about them makes you avoid unexpected pitfalls when developing the conceptual (theoretical) framework of your study. This way you lend credibility to your problem. The more aware you are of the gaps in studies already conducted, the more careful you would be in planning things.

- It helps identify general patterns to findings from multiple examples of research in the same area, thereby keeping you on guards against any duplication and unproductive activity, thus enabling you economize on your precious resources.
- Literature review assists in exploring explanations and discrepancies by juxtaposing studies with apparently conflicting findings. This way you are able to develop a sort of link between the known and the yet-to-be-known.
- It helps define your terminology or identify variations in definitions used by researchers or practitioners.
- It enables you to identify appropriate research methodologies. Bookwalter & Bookwalter (1968) aptly remark: "Not only does he (the researcher) need to know what has been done in the subject area, but he also knows the degree of success that was found in the use of the research techniques or methods." So, being forewarned is to be forearmed.
- Literature review helps you identify validated specific techniques, scales and instruments that ensure success which you deserve. In other words, it makes you more confident and courageous in facing the challenges.

8

Research Proposal, Meaning and Significance of Research Proposal

Research proposal is otherwise called as "Synopsis" According to Sidhu and Singh, "It is the logical and systematic planning of a piece of Research". It is in the form of a blue print or an outline, which indicates the border of study, its orientation, the methodology, the line of approach and its scope.

The preparation of a research proposal, synopsis, or plan is prerequisite in the research process. In many institutions a researcher is required to submit the same for its approval. This serves as a basis for determining the feasibility of the project and provides a systematic plan of procedure for the researcher to follow. It also gives the research supervisors a basis for guiding the research in the smooth conduct of the research. After selecting an appropriate research problem, the research scholar has to submit a research proposal to the institution or university to get the problem approved. The proposal should be good enough to convince the committee that the problem is important and worth investigating. Basically, the research proposal contains the definition, scope, significance of the problem, a brief review of related literature, and the methodology that will be used to solve it.

The preparation of a research proposal is very important in any research process. It is like a blueprint that an architect prepares before the construction of a building. The initial draft proposal is subject to modification as and when required. A good research must be carefully planned and systematically carried out.

The research proposal is having the below mentioned parts: —

(1) The statement of the problem.

(2) The significance of the problem.

(3) Definitions assumptions, limitations and delimitations.

(4) Review of related literature.

(5) The hypothesis.

(6) Methods, and procedures.

(7) Time schedule.

(8) Bibliography.

(1) STATEMENT OF THE PROBLEM

The problem should be stated in a clear manner. Normally, it will be a declarative statement but it may be in the question form. It should also indicate whether the study is comparative, normative or experimental. The researcher can state the cause and effect relationship between the variables in the study. A clear statement of problem speaks thousands of words about the researcher's experience, maturity, knowledge and intellectual calibre For e.g.

(1) Participation in the high school competition are detrimental to academic achievements.

(2) Children who have had kindergarten experience may show a greater academic achievement in the first grade than those with no experience.

These statements suggests the answers or conclusions and provide a focus for research activity.

(2) THE SIGNIFICANCE OF THE PROBLEM

The scope and importance of the study must be clearly mentioned. The researcher must state clearly that who will be benefited from the study and how will the result and conclusions i.e. findings influence the present policies and practices in the field of physical education and sports? Will it be worthful as regards the cost and efforts spent on it? The answers for all these questions must be given.

(3) DEFINITIONS, ASSUMPTIONS, LIMITATIONS AND DELIMITATIONS

Definitions— It is very important to define all the unusual terms that may be misinterpreted. The operational definitions of the terms are very important than the mere dictionary meaning. For e.g., athlete, physical fitness, speed, power, intelligence, the ball games, indoor activities, rhythemic activities etc.

Assumptions :— Assumptions are the statements of what the investigator believes with the careful observations, a researcher can assume about various facts or aspects.

Limitations :— Limitations are the conditions and factors beyond the control of the researcher. These limitations must be mentioned in the proposal or the blue-print. The limitations that may place restrictions on the conclusions of the study and their applications to other situations must be mentioned or avoid using more than one class in an experiment, a data gathering instrument that has not been validated or the inability in the random selection and assignment of subjects to the experimental and control groups etc., are the examples of limitations.

Delimitations :— These are the boundaries of the study. The number of the subject, sex, age, the variables included etc., should be specified. Even the area and the period also must be mentioned.

(4) REVIEW OF RELATED LITERATURE

The related literature must be reviewed, because it helps the researcher in stating what is already known and what is unknown. It also helps the researcher in making concepts clear, to formulate hypothesis and provides the directions. It helps in developing the background story. It should be briefed to the point.

The reference should include information regarding design, sample and sampling, instruments used for the collection of data, the variables included etc. That will help the researcher in proceeding with less studies.

(5) THE HYPOTHESIS

The hypothesis is a tentative answer to the questions or it is an intelligent **guess**. Hypothesis must be formulated before the collection of data. A good hypothesis should have the following characteristics :—

(a) It should be reasonable.

(b) It should be consistant with known facts and theories.

(c) It should be stated in such a way that it can be tested and found to be probably true or probably false.

(d) It should be stated in simplest possible form.

The hypothesis formulated before the collection of data helps researcher by avoiding the researcher by unbiased investigation.

(6) METHODS AND PROCEDURES

This part of the research proposal is very highly technical and should be written very carefully. The investigator has to clearly state how he proposes to investigate the problem including samples and sampling technique, what are the instruments or tools he employs for the gathering of the data, what statistical procedures would be adopted to process, analyse and interpret the data, how the conclusions would be drawn.

(7) TIME-SCHEDULE

A time schedule should be prepared by the researcher so that it will help him to budget his time and energy effectively. It helps the researcher in completion of his study systematically. He should fix up the probable dates for all the part of the investigation. i.e.,

(a) For the submission of the proposal.

(b) For the review of the literature.

(c) For the collection of the data.

(d) For analysing and interpretation of the data.

(e) For arriving at the conclusion and writing the report.

(f) For the submission of the final report and so on.

BIBLIOGRAPHY

At the end, the researcher should provide the list of authors he has referred for his study, which is called as bibliography. The reference should be arranged in an alphabetical order. The bibliography will provide an opportunity to the researcher to acknowledge the authors indebtedness about the sources.

Types

Research proposals may be solicited, meaning they are submitted in response to a request with specified requirements, such as an RFP, or they may be unsolicited, meaning they are submitted without prior request. Other types of proposals include "preproposals", where a letter of intent or brief abstract is submitted for review prior to submission of a full proposal; continuation proposals, which re-iterate an original proposal and its funding requirements in order to ensure continued funding; and renewal proposals, which seek continued sponsorship of a project which would otherwise be terminated.

Academic research proposals are generally written as part of the initial requirements of writing a thesis, research paper, or dissertation. They generally follow the same format as a research paper, with an introduction, a literature review, a discussion of research methodology and goals, and a conclusion. This basic structure may vary between projects and between fields, each of which may have its own requirements.

An explanation of the significance of a study may include the meaning of the research work to you personally and should include how your research benefits or impacts others in part or whole. Discuss what people or groups of people might benefit from reading your research. Show how this project is significant to developing a body of knowledge. If your investigation will contribute to a portion of a larger investigation, describe that larger investigation as well.

This section, often referred to as the "rationale" is crucial, because it is one place in which the researcher tries to convince an audience that the research is worth doing and could persuade someone to support, or fund, a research project.

One way to do this is by describing how the results may be used. This is where your purpose for research, a decision that you made earlier when you composed your research proposal statement, becomes very important. The purpose for your research may also be incorporated into your thinking about the purpose for your investigation, too.

Remember...

- If you are doing basic research, then you are doing research to construct new knowledge for the sake of theory. Its design is not controlled by the practical usefulness of the findings. It is experimental and theoretical work undertaken to acquire new knowledge without looking for long-term benefits other than the advancement of knowledge.

- If you are doing applied research, then you are doing research to show how the findings can be applied or summarized into some type of methodology in order to solve practical problems.

- If you are doing practical research, then you are going one step beyond applied research and applying the findings of your research to a specific "practical" situation like an action research project or a clinical trial.

The purpose for your research is part of what makes your research significant.

Consider the following questions to help you decide what your research investigation's is:

- Why is this work important?
- What are the implications of doing it?
- How does it link to other knowledge?
- How does it stand to inform policy making? Save money? Improve or reduce something?
- Why is it important to our understanding of the world?
- What new perspective will you bring to the topic?
- What use might your final research paper have for others in this field or in the general public?
- Who might you decide to share your findings with once the project is complete?

Think about how your research:

- may resolve lingering questions or gaps in knowledge in your field of study
- may develop better theoretical models in your area
- may influence public policy
- may change the way people do their jobs in a particular field, or may change the way people live.

Are there other contributions your research will make? If so, describe them in detail.

SIGNIFICANCE OF RESEARCH PROPOSAL

What is Research Proposal? It is very important to understand. Mostly, students who are new in the field of research or beginners, don't understand fully what it actually means. A research proposal needs to be good as ones research. A research proposal is a proposal through which you need to convince others that you have great research idea and have the required abilities to complete it on time. The evaluators evaluate your proposed study through the proposal. So, it should have necessary information and key elements on the basis of which it could be evaluated.. Sometimes a good research project is been rejected due to poorly written research proposal, so quality of your research writing matters a lot along with the quality of your proposed research.

Points you need to focus on while writing a research proposal:

(1) Title: Title should be short and descriptive. An informative and catchy title will not only creates interest but also persuade the readers favorably towards the proposal.

(2) Abstract: It is defined as a small summary of around about 300 words, which should include the research problem, basis for the study, assumption if have any, methods and findings.

(3) Introduction: In an introduction part you need to introduce your research problem, provide the necessary background for it. Framing a problem is in itself a toughest task. As such there is no particular format for framing your research question, all depends upon your creativity, ability to think independently and the understanding you have towards your research area .You need to bring out the importance of your research area in front of your readers. Introduction generally covers following points:

(i) Research problem

(ii) Provide the context/background for your research problem.

(iii) Rationale for the research study

(iv) Discussing major and minor issues mentioned in your research.

(v) Identification of dependent and independent variables.

(vi) Assumption ,if any

Literature View

It is a summary and explanation of key studies relevant to a proposed project. You need to showcase the stage for your work and how your piece of work is going to benefit. It reveals many important functions like your ability to analyze and evaluate relevant literature information, provides new insights etc.

You can organize your review in different ways but it should be presentable and systematic for example: you can make use subheading under main heading.

Method: This section tells the research committee about your plan of action i.e., the way you will solve your research problem.

So, it is imperative part of your research proposal. In the method section you need to provide adequate information and should be able to proof that your approach is the most pertinent and suitable, to solve out your research problem.

Results: At this phase, it is very obvious that you don't have any results but you should recapitulate what you expect to generate during the course of your research and impacts that you expect from it to have.

Significance of the research problem refers to its purpose(s), i.e. the contribution it will make to human welfare and human education. Under this sub-head, the researcher is obliged to answer such pertinent questions as Will the results of the study make a difference that matters to (physical education as) a profession, a programme of activity and an academic discipline? How will the study add to the field of knowledge - sport education and/or spot sciences? Will the findings of the study help improve policies and practices in physical education and sports, and if yes, how? Will the study generate further interest among research community for more varied studies on the issue? Will it raise researchers' competencies and coax them adopt more innovative approach in methodological techniques? Will the study contribute to supporting or building a theory? Will it really be worth the cost and energy expended? and so on. The underlying message in this regard should be loud and clear.

Objectives of the Study

It is not possible to visualize a research study without an objective. The researcher should do well to provide a clear statement on the overall question, in other words, the general objectives of the problem. Then he should follow it with action-oriented tasks, i.e. specific objectives. If the specific objectives are more than one, they should be cited (briefly explained) sequentially.

Definition of Important (or Technical) Terms

Important concepts, variables or abstract terms, which are the main stay of the study, need to be defined in their operational nuances (i.e. in the sense they are used in the study) in order to enable the reader to understand what actually these mean in that context. Concrete variables like temperature, heart beat, respiratory rate, weight, time, oxygen consumption, etc., standard definitions, which are accepted as such in almost all contexts. But abstract concepts and variables like intelligence, personality, confidence, motivation or anxiety have no standard definition. Their meaning change from context to context.To overcome this hurdle, the researcher would need to develop (use) some system of measurement, for example, a Likert scale (from '1- strongly disagree', to '5 - strongly agree') to measure responses on a questionnaire quantitatively. If intelligence, for instance, is measured through IQ , then this would be its operational definition.

In research, the operational definition of a concept is important, not its dictionary meaning or encyclopaedic explanation. According to Stangor (1998), operational definition of a term refers to "a precise statement of how a conceptual variable is turned into a measured variable". As a matter fact, the operational definition of a significant term "is one that you can come back to a day, a week, or a year later and understand and use in the same manner...." (Schweigert,1994). In physical education and sports, the terms like athlete, sport, fitness, intelligence, skill, scores, etc., may be household words but not easy to define operationally due to fluidity in their meanings. In research context, they must be defined in terms of the operations or processes that will be used to measure or manipulate these concepts or variables. For instance, a score on a standardized test of intelligence may offer a better operational definition of intelligence than a conceptual definition or explanation given to it by Binet or Thurstone. To avoid confusion, only one operational definition of each variable or concept would be sufficient.

Review of Related Literature

Besides, personal experience and academic (scientific) interaction with the experts in the field, literature review is the major source of developing a research problem. It is a process of reading, analysing, evaluating, and summarizing scholarly materials about a specific topic, which enables the researcher to (a) define the limits of the field; (b) explain abstract concepts operationally; (c) formulate hypothesis; and (d) establish his credibility as a scholar of the knowledge domain. Literature review, according to Fink (2009), is a sort of "subjective examination of recorded information," for purposes listed above. When doing a research review, you systematically examine all sources and describe and justify what you are going to do or have done.

In a research proposal citing studies and authors is limited and is done mainly to develop the conceptual framework or rationale of the study. When citing studies, the reference information should include design of the study, characteristics of the subjects, sampling techniques, data sources, and instruments used for data collection; variables that were identified and manipulated, and the extraneous factors that could affect the findings; faults that could have been avoided, and the recommendations for further studies.

Procedure or Methodology

Methodology to be adopted has a unique place in the study for its criticality. Therefore, it must be stated very explicitly. It should cover enough detail so that the reader can follow it without any hassle. Under this sub-head the researcher must briefly explain the complete procedure from A to Z sequentially and systematically. It starts with an overall summary of the study design and methodological approach, followed by methodology for each specific objective. The description as such should include (a) the specific design (what you will do and how, number of replicates, etc.); (b) the materials (instruments, tools, subject sample) and techniques (of sampling, tool selection, data collection, data treatment) to be used; and (c) feasibility of the techniques. It would be economical and effective to use literature to support design, materials & techniques. It is naive to repeat standard procedures; just give a reference. The researcher should do well to rationally and convincingly explain his preferences and priorities for particular variables, techniques, treatments, tools and materials, and literature citation.

Bibliography

The research proposal document ends with bibliography or references to the authors/works consulted and cited to develop and strengthen the base of the research question and the study. As a matter of principle , the more selective the bibliography, the better. In education, psychology and physical education, the APA format of bibliography is preferred.

9

Preparation of Research Proposal/Project

The research conducted must be reported properly, otherwise the most brilliant hypothesis generalisations, the best organised studies will be of no use. According to *Manroe* and Englehaart, "The report of an investigation, not only serves to record and communicate, but it also fulfils an important function in the process of research".

CHARACTERISTICS OF A GOOD RESEARCH REPORT

All the reports may not be same, they may differ considerably. Even then, some of the basic characteristics have been given below:

(1) The research report must be clear in expression of ideas and facts.

(2) Right choice of words, sentences, idioms, phrases, must be done.

(3) The entire material of research should be properly organised.

(4) The material should be presented in a standardise and acceptable form. The tables, diagrams, graphs must be standard one.

(5) The research report must be complete in all respects.

(6) The report must indicate the capacity, competency, proficiency etc. of the researcher.

PARTS OF THE RESEARCH REPORT OR FORMAT OF RESEARCH REPORT

Although the research reports may differ considerably, a particular format is given below –

(1) Preliminary section or Front material :–

(a) Title page

(b) Approval page

(c) Dedication

(d) Vita or biodata of the author
(e) Acknowledgement
(f) Table of contents
(g) List of tables
(h) List of figures.

(2) Main body of the report

(A) Introduction

(i) Statement of the problem
(ii) Significance of the problem
(iii) Definition of important terms, assumptions, limitations and delimitations
(iv) Hypothesis.

(B) Review of related literatures :–

(C) Design of the study

(i) Procedures used
(ii) Subjects, and sampling technique followed
(iii) Method of collecting the data
(iv) Description of tools or instruments.

(D) Presentation, analysis and interpretation of data

(i) Data
(ii) Tables
(iii) Figures.

(E) Summery and conclusion

(i) Summary of the procedure followed
(ii) The main findings and conclusions
(iii) Recommendations for further study.

(3) Supplementary material or Back material

(i) Bibliography
(ii) Appendix
(iii) Index
(iv) Footnote.

(1) PRELIMINARY SECTION OR FRONT MATERIAL

(a) **The title page** – The first page of the thesis is known as the title page. It should include, the title of the study, name of investigator, name of the institution where it is submitted, name of the degree, name of the supervisor or guide under whose guidance the study was completed. The title should be typed or printed in bold letters in a reverse pyramid shape.

(b) **Approval page** – One page should be provided for the approval or certificate by the supervisor or guide.

(c) **Dedication** – It is an optional one. Some investigators may dedicate their work to their beloveds like parents, teachers, wife/husband, son/daughter, etc. It is nothing but an expression of gratitude, love and affection.

(d) **Vita** – The biodata of the investigator i.e., name, qualification, experience, etc. should be included.

(e) **Acknowledgement** – It is nothing but a matter of courtesy and indebtedness towards the help and guidance he has taken from the guide, supervisor, other faculty members, seniorns, and other friends during the completion of his work.

(f) **Table of contents** – Chapter headings, major sub divisions, some times the topics within the sub divisions etc. with their page numbers must be given in the table of contents. It helps the readers to go directly to the concerned topic without wasting time for searching.

(g) **List of tables** – If the tables appear in the thesis, they must be listed on a separate page and should be placed next to the table of contents.

(h) **List of figures** – If the illustrations and figures are shown in the thesis, a seperate list of them also should be given.

Chapter headings must be typed in capital letters, sub divisions in small letters, list of tables in Roman numbers and list of figures should be numbered in Arabic numerals.

(2) MAIN BODY OF THE REPORT

The main body of the report includes all the chapters which are explained below –

(A) Introduction :–

(i) **Statement of the problem** – The problem should be stated in a clear cut and logical manner. The reader should be able to get the clear idea about the study.

(ii) **Significance of the problem** – The need, importance, and scope of the study must be mentioned. The justification of the study is developed by giving the significance.

(iii) **Definition of important terms, assumptions, limitations and delimitations** – The investigator should define all the important and unusual terms used in the statement of the problem. It gives the reader a clear concept. For e.g., school boys school, girls school, co-educational, residential, non-residential, etc. sports, games, athletics, competitions etc.

Assumptions – Assumptions are nothing but the beliefs of the investigator, they also must be stated.

Limitations and delimitations – The factors beyond the control of the investigator are called as limitations and the boundaries for the study irrespective of area, period, sex etc. are the delimitations. The researcher should explain his limitations and the delimitations of the readers.

(iv) **Hypothesis** – Hypothesis are formulated by the experience and evidence available. Here also the investigator will assume and hope something about the investigation. Normally hypothesis will provide a direction for the study. For some studies like case study, construction of norms, etc. there will be no hypothesis at all.

(B) **Review of related literature** – Abstracts or findings of previous research related to the topic are quoted. This will provide a back ground for the development of the present study. A brief summary of studies regarding agreement and disagreement, or the gap in the existing knowledge must be included.

(C) **Design of the study** – The procedure employed in the study regarding the sample and sampling technique, the variables considered, the tools used for the collection of data, the statistical procedure used for tabulation and analysis of the data, the tests conducted, etc. all must be explained.

(D) **Presentation, analysis and interpretation** – This part is considered as the heart of the research report. The data collected should be properly presented and clear explanation regarding analysis and interpretation of the data should be given. The data should be systematically arranged in tables and wherever necessary, the figures must be given.

(E) **Summery and conclusion** – This is the most difficult part in writing a report, because all the procedures, findings, conclusions and recommendations also must be given in a summarised and brief manner.

The summery and conclusion part is the most widely read part of the study, because it recapitulates the information that has been presented in previous sections of the report. The investigator must recommend for the further research in the similar field.

(3) Supplementary material or back material

After the main body of the report, the bibliography, appendix and index should be given. This part is called as back material or supplementary material.

(a) **The bibliography** – The bibliography should include all references of books, journals, magazines and bulletins etc. The bibliography should be written, alphabatically with the authors last name. If more number of books written by same author have been referred, all those references should be arranged alphabetically by the title under the author's name. If the book was jointly written by more number of authors; the main author's (first given) name should be written and 'et al' or 'and others' should be written.

If the same work is cited again, then it is indicated by ibid followed by a comma and page number. Single page is indicated by p., and more number of pages pp.

After the author's name, the title of the book, name of publisher's and year of publication should be written. If the book has got more number of editions, then the edition number also must be written.

(b) **Appendix** – It is not merely dumping the left over material, but it should be a supporting material which can not be placed in the main body.

(c) **Index** – The subject index in an alphabetical order should be given at the last, which is helpful for the reader's to find the important matter or subject immediately.

Footnoting – Foot notes are meant for the cross references. They are placed or numbered consequently, usually starting with 1 for each chapter. Numbers should be put slightly above the line normally at the end of citation. And at the foot of the page, the foot note number will be written and then the author's name, title of the book, publisher's name and address, year of publication and the page number should be written. Foot notes have to be typed with single space and if more foot notes are to be written double space should be used in between two foot notes and the foot note should be typed with small letters (small size).

10

Research Report

A research report is a document prepared by an analyst or strategist who is a part of the investment research team in a stock brokerage or investment bank. A research report may focus on a specific stock or industry sector, a currency, commodity or fixed-income instrument, or on a geographic region or country. Research reports generally, but not always, have actionable recommendations such as investment ideas that investors can act upon. Writing and reporting makes research studies more trustworthy and credible; their conclusions are remembered more accurately and understood better in the light of the facts highlighted with vehemence; and they extend a helping hand to a wide variety of concerned individuals - scientists, young researchers, teachers, physical educators, coaches, sport scientists, administrators, athletes, and so on. Research reports are not creative writings, opinion pieces, poems, novels, letters, musings, memoirs, or interesting to read; they are rational description of empirical data generated through actual testing and measurement of variables under natural and/or controlled conditions as the case may be.

Hence they may be insipid and uninteresting to common multitude but highly valuable to the learned because they communicate a set of ideas and facts either brought into existence afresh or interpreted in new ways through empirical and/or rational research strategies. The most brilliant hypotheses, theories, generalizations and studies become meaningless entities unless reported in a smart way, and communicated to those who seek them and give them a meaning. A report aims to inform, as clearly and succinctly as possible. As a matter of principle, the research report must be written and published so that (a) its findings are known to and believed by those who would like to add to their wisdom; (b) something more is added to the existing knowledge base; (c) new research gets underway in the concerned knowledge domain; (d) there is further exploration of ideas; and (e) refinement takes places in procedures of research and the technology applied to it. It needs no reiteration that dissemination of research findings is the end goal of all research and research reporting is a professional obligation for the researcher and he must discharge it in the interest of the society. It mutually benefits the researcher and the society. Report writing is an essential skill for professionals. Writing research report is both a science and an art. It is science because what is reported is very precise, to-the-point and systematic with no room for ifs and buts; it is art because the expression of ideas (the facts) is as artistic and bewitching as slick floor acrobats of an artistic female gymnast.

The approach to writing research report varies from discipline to discipline. A literary research report, an observational research report and an experimental research report are naturally at variance in expression and writing style. A report is similar to an essay in that both need (a) a formal writing style; (b) both have an introduction, body and conclusion; (c) analytical thinking is deeply involved in both; and (d) both require neat presentation. However, the major difference between the two is that a research report presents an information, not an argument and its is meant to be scanned quickly by the reader. Exactly what you include in your report and how you present it will vary according to your discipline and the specific purpose of the report.

According to some researchers and anaylists there is some similarity between cooking and research report writing. Both need meticulous preparation. As in cooking, so in research reporting, keep everything (your notes, literature review, processed data, references, graphics, bibliography, etc.) in readiness at hand before you actually begin to pen down even the first sentence of the report. Preparing a research report involves other activities besides writing; in fact, writing is actually the last step in the preparation process. Before writing can take place, the results of the research project must be fully understood and thought must be given to what the report will say. Thus, preparing a research report involves three steps: understanding, organising and writing. The following hints might be useful to you in getting started:

1. Write in an academic style and tone. Use a formal objective

style. Usually avoid personal pronouns, for example, "I observed....." If in doubt, check with your supervisor or any other expert.

2. Do not worry too much about the final form and language, but rather on presenting the ideas coherently and logically.

3. Develop an outline of the report showing appropriate divisions and subdivisions. This may be expanded into a brief of the study containing reference material, data, results, conclusions, points of discussion, etc., in a sequential order. Make sure that nothing of importance is left out. Revise, revise, revise, revise and revise again. Move forward-backward in time and space to write and revise before you feel satisfied with your effort.

4. Better type out the draft report before passing it on to the professional computer type-setter for onward action. This will reduce chances of printer's devil and ensure a better getup of the report.

5. At the outset, familiarize yourself with the research report format as followed in your discipline or faculty. You may consult authoritative literature, your supervisor and, if need be, other knowledgeable persons famous for their expertise in report writing.

6. From this brief (outline), now develop the initial draft of the report which might need several revisions before emerging as the finished product. Some last minute changes and adjustments in format, reference material, illustrations and result discussion may not be ruled out. This may, at times, be tiring but, by all means, satisfying and encouraging.

7. Communicate the main ideas followed by supporting details and examples. Start with the more important or significant information and move on to the least important information. Do not expect perfection right at the start. Be prepared to junk whole sections because every time you pause while writing, your inner self suggests some change, which you are bound to follow. Try to discover new insights while writing.

8. Writing is an iterative process. So you don't have to start at the beginning. Whatever you do, just start writing, jumping headlong into the deep waters. The first sentence itself will be difficult to come out but once it is appears in black and white, then there would not stopping.

GENERAL GUIDELINES FOR RESEARCH REPORT

No hard and fast rules exist for research report writing. Most procedures of writing a research report are directed by conviction, convention, and convenience. As a matter of fact, every individual has a different style of writing. There is not really one right style for a report, but there definitely are some clear basic principles for a research report writing.

- A good research report is marked by clarity. All significant ideas and facts pertaining to the research question and conclusions of the report must be presented in a clear and straightforward manner - one idea automatically leading to another.

- Since language is a vehicle of thought and a medium of thought expression, it is necessary to make an appropriate choice of words, sentences, phrases and idioms to express facts, idea and views. A simple, idiomatic, direct and meaningful language will accomplish this objective more easily than an alliterative, pedantic and bombastic one.

- In no case, should the report sound overly personal, but rather objective both in content and diction. Customarily, the report should be written in past tense, passive voice and in third person. Sexist language and words having double meaning should be avoided at all costs.

- The information in the report should be organized logically with appropriate chapterization, thereby helping the reader to know the worth of the document at first sight itself. Each chapter should be distinctively demarcated in terms of content. Content overlapping is least permissible.

- The material should be presented in a standard and acceptable format as prevalent in the discipline (or under the Faculty) in which the study is conducted. The data should be illustrated using suitable, attractive and well-designed graphics, tables, pictorials, photographs, and diagrams. This will give the report a striking outlook and add to its internal beauty.

- The data may be presented in descriptive, comparative or correlational form depending on the nature of the study - experimental or historical- and the type of data generated. Statistics used for treatment of data have much to do with their presentation, and style and diction of the report.

• On the one hand, the report should be complete in the sense that it stands by itself and that no additional clarification is needed. On the other hand, the report must be concise and must focus on the critical elements of the project and must exclude unimportant issues. All significant ideas with appropriate comments, interpretations and explanations should find place in it. The report must cogently and rationally explain how gap in knowledge was found, how research question has been addressed in order to close the gap, what hurdles were encountered in sampling, data collection, controlling extraneous variables, etc., and how they were overcome, and finally whether there is any semblance between the known facts and derived conclusions. A good report should never leave any significant question on the topic unanswered.

• The report should, by and large, reflect the researcher's reflectivity, erudition, wisdom, and intellectual competence. A good researcher is known by how he convincingly conveys to the reader what he has researched.

In format, the research proposal and the research report stand at par except that the proposal indicates what is proposed to be done and the report expounds what has been accomplished and how. If you had prepared very astutely, you will find research report writing a left-handed job.

NORMAL FORMAT OF RESEARCH REPORT

A research report or thesis is typically made up of three main divisions: (1) preliminary division or front matter, (2) main body of the report, and (3) supplementary (end) matter. Each of the divisions and sections contains a categorically different kind of content.

The Front Matter

Preliminary (or front) matter is all that come before the main body of the report. It is a sort of introduction to the investigation to the research question.

Title

The title page gives the first impression of the report. It should carry the caption or heading of the research question, the researcher's name, his or her institutional affiliation, the name of the institution (university) where the report is submitted for assessment for a degree, the date of presentation and, if necessary, name of the researcher's supervisor. The title should be printed in an attractive style in bold letters on the top of the page with equal margin on the sides with rest of the matter placed properly. Expert binders know how to typeset the title page in style. You need to be extra cautious about spelling each word of the title correctly without even missing or misplacing the punctuation signs. A flawless and interesting or amusing title impresses all and sundry and speaks volumes about the researchers' standing.

Preface or Acknowledgments

Preface is not a requirement in the research report. However, it is customary for the researcher to shed some light on their personal interests and experiences briefly and also express their gratitude in a short paragraph to all those who substantially contributed to the collection of data and completion of the study. Importantly, one should be neither too lavish nor too frugal in acknowledging the indebtedness and thankfulness. Flattering seniors, colleagues, professors, departmental heads, etc., beyond the limits of reasonability will be no less than stooping too low to conquer. Every researcher should guard against it.

List of Contents

This is a list of the headings and appendices of the report. It should spread over two pages. Depending on the complexity and length of the report, you could list tables, figures and appendices separately as they appear in sequence. Make sure the correct page numbers are shown opposite the contents. Up-to-date word processing packages can generate a table of contents for you.

List of Tables

List of tables is given separately and not mixed with the tables of contents. Exact page number on which the table(s) appear should be given.

List of Figures

Like the list of tables, the list of figures should also be given separately. The figures should be numbered continuously and the page number cited in each case.

Conventionally, the preliminary section of the research report should be paged in lower case Roman numerals e.g. i, ii, iii, iv, etc.

Selected References

Best, John W. (1983) *Research in Education* (4th Ed.). New Delhi; Prentice Hall of India.

Bookwalter, Carolyn; Bookwalter, Carl; & Phillips, Marjorie (1968) Writing the research report. In M. Gladys Scott (ed.) *Research Methods in health, physical education recreation*, Washington, D.C., American Association for Health, Physical Education, and Recreation.

Clarke, David H. & Clarke, H. Harrison (1970) *Research processes in physical education, recreation and health*. Englewood Cliffs, NJ; Prentice Hall.

Kamlesh M.L., *Methodology of Research in Physical Education and Sports*, Metropolitan India, 1986.

Kutty, S.K., *Research Methodology*, 2015, Sports Publication, New Delhi.

Moorthy. A. M., "*Research Methods in Physical Education, Sports and Exercise Sciences*". Friends Publications, New Dehli 2000.

Ryce, J.R. & Powell, D. (1993) *Theory of personality and individual differences : factors, systems and processes*. Englewood Cliffs, N.J.; Simon and Schuster, Prentice Hall.

Schweigert, Wendy A. (1994) *Research methods and statistics for psychology*. Pacific Grove, California; Books/Cole.

Sprinthall, Richard C., Sehmutte, Gregory T., & Cirois, Lee (1991) *Understanding educational research*. Englewood Cliffs, N.J..

Stangor, Charles (1998) *Research methods for the behavioral sciences*. Boston; Houghton Miffin.

Vastrad, B., *Methodology of Research in Physical Education and Sports*., Khel Sahitya Kendra, New Delhi.

UNIT- 3
Basics of Statistical Analysis

11

Statistics: Meaning, Definition, Nature and Importance

MEANING AND DEFINITION OF STATISTICS

The term "statistics" is used in two senses : first in plural sense meaning a collection of numerical facts or estimates—the figure themselves. It is in this sense that the public usually think of statistics, e.g., figures relating to population, profits of different units in an industry etc. Secondly, as a singular noun, the term'statistics' denotes the various methods adopted for the collection, analysis and interpretation of the factsnumerically represented. In singular sense, the term 'statistics' is better described as statistical methods. In our study of the subject, we shall be more concerned with the second meaning of the word 'statistics'.

During last few years statistics have assumed a significant role in Physical Education and Sports. Using statistics in the research articles to infer the findings have become a very common feature. But somehow or other this area is still in its infancy stage as far as its application in sports research is concerned. Often, the scholar has a confusion that one who does not have a mathematical background cannot make a dent in this area. In fact what is expected from the professionals is to appreciate the concept of various statistical techniques for better understanding and viewing correctly the problems encountered in sports research.

Statistics provide us a scientific basis to our inferences drawn from experimental results. Before discussing the various aspects of it let us see what statistics does ? and what its purpose is ? Consider an experiment in which we are interested to investigate, whether 6 weeks aerobic work-out increases haemoglobin counts in the college girls ? Naturally all the college girls cannot be taken under study, so we resort to a representative sample on which aerobic workout is administered. After counting the haemoglobin counts before and after experiment, an appropriate statistical test is applied. If the test suggests that there is a significant improvement in the count, this inference needs to be generalised for the entire college girls. However, various factors like representativeness of the sample, reliability in the measurement of haemoglobin counts and choosing the correct statistical techniques will have to be kept in mind. But with some degree of reliability inference could be generalised for the bigger group or population. Thus, the objective of the statistics is to generalise an inference about a population based on the information contained in a sample.

Statistics has been defined differently by different authors and each author has assigned new limits to the field which should be included in its scope. We can do no better than give selected definitions of statistics by some authors and then come to the conclusion about the scope of the subject.

A.L. Bowley defines, "Statistics may be called the science of counting". At another place he defines, "Statistics may be called the science of averages". Both these definitions are narrow and throw light only on one aspect of Statistics.

According to King, "The science of statistics is the method of judging collective, natural or social, phenomenon from the results obtained from the analysis or enumeration or collection of estimates".

Many a time counting is not possible and estimates are required to be made. Therefore, Boddington defines it as "the science of estimates and probabilities". But this definition also does not cover the entire scope of statistics. The statistical methods are methods for the collection, analysis and interpretation of numerical data and form a basis for the analysis and comparison of the observed phenomena. In the words of Croxton &Cowden, "Statistics may be defined as the collection, presentation, analysis and interpretation of numericaldata".

Horace Secrist has given an exhaustive definition of the term satistics in the plural sense. According to him:

"By statistics we mean aggregates of facts affected to a marked extent by a multiplicity of causesnumerically expressed, enumerated or estimated according to reasonable standards of accuracy collected in a systematic manner for a pre-determined purpose and placed in relation to each other".

This definition makes it quite clear that as numerical statement of facts, 'statistic' should possess thefollowing characteristics.

1. **Statistics are aggregate of facts**

A single age of 20 or 30 years is not statistics, a series of ages are. Similarly, a single figure relating to production, sales, birth, death etc., would not be statistics although aggregates of such figures would bestatistics because of their comparability and relationship.

2. Statistics are affected to a marked extent by a multiplicity of causes

A number of causes affect statistics in a particular field of enquiry, e.g., in production statistics are affected by climate, soil, fertility, availability of raw materials and methods of quick transport.

3. Statistics are numerically expressed, enumrated or estimated

The subject of statistics is concerned essentially with facts expressed in numerical form—with theirquantitative details but not qualitative descriptions. Therefore, facts indicated by terms such as 'good', 'poor' are not statistics unless a numerical equivalent, is assigned to each expression. Also this may either beenumerated or estimated, where actual enumeration is either not possible or is very difficult.

4. Statistics are numerated or estimated according to reasonable standard of accuracy

Personal bias and prejudices of the enumeration should not enter into the counting or estimation of figures, otherwise conclusions from the figures would not be accurate. The figures should be counted or estimated according to reasonable standards of accuracy. Absolute accuracy is neither necessary nor sometimes possible in social sciences. But whatever standard of accuracy is once adopted, should be used throughout the process of collection or estimation.

5. Statistics should be collected in a systematic manner for a predetermined purpose

The statistical methods to be applied on the purpose of enquiry since figures are always collected with some purpose. If there is no predetermined purpose, all the efforts in collecting the figures may prove to be wasteful. The purpose of a series of ages of husbands and wives may be to find whether young husbands have young wives and the old husbands have old wives.

6. Statistics should be capable of being placed in relation to each other

The collected figure should be comparable and well-connected in the same department of inquiry. Ages of husbands are to be compared only with the corresponding ages of wives, and not with, say, heights of trees.

NATURE AND IMPORTANCE OF STATISTICS

NATURE OF STATISTICS

Statistics is the study of numerical information called data. Statisticians acquire, study and formulate conclusions based on data they collect using any of several different methods.

As a science, it studies the statistics in a systematic manner. As an art, it uses statistics to solve the problems of real life. But it is not a complete science such as Physics and Chemistry. Because in these all the causes are kept under control and the observations and results are found similar. But such is not the case with statistics, because observations are made and results are found, but in the mean time situations change so result also change.

"Statistics-A New Approach" have stated that "Statistics is not a body of substantive knowledge but a body of methods for obtaining knowledge." —Wallis and Roberts.

Subject Matter

Here we go through all the laws, by laws, rules, sub-rules and general principles. These include collection, organisation, presentation, analysis and interpretation of data relating to the inquiry. This has already been elaborated.

"By statistical methods, we mean methods especially adopted for elucidation of quantitative data affected by multiplicity of causes." —Yule and Kendall

Applied Statistics:

This can be classified into two parts:

(i) Descriptive and

(ii) Scientific

(i) deals with the data those have been collected and

(ii) deals with the formation of laws those are based upon above data.

Characteristics of Statistics

The following are the general characteristics of statistics:

1. Statistics are numerated or estimated according to reasonable standard of accuracy

Personal bias and prejudices of the enumeration should not enter into the counting or estimation of figures, otherwise conclusions from the figures would not be accurate. The figures should be counted or estimated according to reasonable standards of accuracy. Absolute accuracy is neither necessary nor sometimes possible in social sciences. But whatever standard of accuracy is once adopted, should be used throughout the process of collection or estimation.

2. Statistics are aggregate of facts

A single age of 20 or 30 years is not statistics, a series of ages are. Similarly, a single figure relating to production, sales, birth, death etc., would not be statistics although aggregates of such figures would bestatistics because of their comparability and relationship.

3. Statistics should be capable of being placed in relation to each other

The collected figure should be comparable and well-connected in the same department of inquiry. Ages of husbands are to be compared only with the corresponding ages of wives, and not with, say, heights of trees.

4. Statistics are numerically expressed, enumrated or estimated

The subject of statistics is concerned essentially with facts expressed in numerical form—with theirquantitative details but not qualitative descriptions. Therefore, facts indicated by terms such as 'good', 'poor' are not statistics unless a numerical equivalent, is assigned to each expression. Also this may either beenumerated or estimated, where actual enumeration is either not possible or is very difficult.

5. Statistics should be collected in a systematic manner for a predetermined purpose

The statistical methods to be applied on the purpose of enquiry since figures are always collected with some purpose. If there is no predetermined purpose, all the efforts in collecting the figures may prove to be wasteful. The purpose of a series of ages of husbands and wives may be to find whether young husbands have young wives and the old husbands have old wives.

6. Statistics are affected to a marked extent by a multiplicity of causes

A number of causes affect statistics in a particular field of enquiry, e.g., in production statistics are affected by climate, soil, fertility, availability of raw materials and methods of quick transport.

IMPORTANCE OF STATISTICS

Any academic discipline cannot grow without advancement of research, so is true with physical education as well. One of the important dimensions of research is the Design of Experiment. Proper statistical design used in a study facilitates us to isolate the factors responsible for the performance on any event. Further, using appropriate statistical design reduces the overall error in the experiment giving more reliable conclusions. New techniques in different sports could be tested with the existing one for better results by using the statistical techniques. For instance, if one has to decide about the duration and type of warm-up exercises before performing 400 meter event in track, it could be inferred by conducting a study in which three or four different types of warm-up exercises could be administered on different group of athletes having homogenous performance. A statistical test used on the 400 meter performance obtained on athletes after exposing them for different warm-up exercises shall facilitate us to choose the best duration and type of warm-up exercise suitable for 400 meter event. Thus development of new techniques and strategy in sports are the results of properly designed experiments based on appropriate statistical techniques. In the development of test battery for measuring motor fitness, athletic fitness, general and specific fitness in different sports, an advance concept of statistical techniques are used. Further, constructing norms for assessing performance on different events is again subject to lot of debates as to which statistical approach is to be adopted for more reliable assessment. If a coach is interested to know about the actual strength of relationships between the performance and independent parameters, partial correlation may be used whereas multiple correlation allows us to find the reliability in estimating the performance based on certain known characteristics. Another area which is very important from the research point of view is to decide about an optimum training load for different levels of athlete. This also requires a lot of statistical intervention.

To measure qualitative characteristics like competitive anxiety, attitude towards sports, knowledge of health education and self concept etc., questionnaire along with their key could be developed. These questionnaires are developed using statistical techniques like difficulty rating and index of discrimination. Further keys may be developed by using some advance statistical techniques like category scale method and factor analysis. All statistical topics mentioned in this chapter shall be discussed in detail in different chapters of the book. Thus we have seen that any advancement in physical education and sports is not possible without statistical application.

Since every academic discipline has different nature of research requirements, therefore physical education too also demands a separate attention from statistical point of view. Looking to the challenge in solving various problems, vast scope of application of statistics in physical education and sports, demands a development of full-fledged discipline as sports statistics.

12

Class Intervals: Raw Score, Continuous and Discrete Series, Class Distribution and Construction of Tables

CLASS INTERVALS: RAW SCORE, CONTINUOUS AND DISCRETE SERIES

When the raw data are presented in a frequency distribution with equal or unequal, inclusive or exclusive class-intervals, we assume that, all the values falling into a particular class-interval are considered to be located at the mid-point (called class-mark) of a class interval. The mid-points of the class interval is obtained by calculating the mean of the lower and the upper limits of the intervals.

$$\text{Mid-point (mid-value)} = \frac{\text{Upper limit} + \text{Lower limit}}{2}$$

(or)

Mid value = lower limit + ½ [size of the class-interaval

Example 1

Calculate the mean of the following frequency distribution:

Class Interval	Frequency
0-8	6
8-16	7
16-24	10
24-32	8
32-40	9

Solution

$$\text{Mid-value} = = \frac{\text{Upper limit} + \text{Lower limit}}{2}$$

Class Interval	Mid-Value x_i	Frequency f_i	Product of f_i and x_i
0-8	4	6	24
8-16	12	7	84
16-24	20	10	200
24-32	28	8	224
32-40	36	9	324
Total		$N = \Sigma f_i = 40$	$\Sigma f_i x_i = 856$

Here $\Sigma f_i = 40$ and $\Sigma f_i x_i = 856$

$$(\bar{x}) = \frac{\sum_{i=1}^{n} f_i x_i}{\Sigma f_i} = \frac{856}{40} = 21.4$$

Mean = 21.4.

Example 2

Calculate the mean of the following frequency distribution

Marks	No. of Students	Marks	No. of Students
10-20	6	50-60	3
20-30	8	60-70	2
30-40	13	70-80	1
40-50	7		

Solution

Marks	Mid-Value x_i	No. of Students f_i	$f_i x_i$
10-20	15	6	90
20-30	25	8	200
30-40	35	13	455
40-50	45	7	315
50-60	55	3	165
60-70	65	2	130
70-80	75	1	75
Total		$N=\Sigma f_i = 40$	$N=\Sigma f_i = 1430$

$$\overline{x} = \frac{1}{N}\sum_{i=1}^{n} f_i x_i = \frac{1430}{40} = 35.75$$

Mean = 35.75.

Rules for Data Sets that Contain a Large Number of Observations

In summary, follow these basic rules when constructing a frequency distribution table for a data set that contains a large number of observations:

- find the lowest and highest values of the variables
- decide on the width of the class intervals
- include all possible values of the variable.

In deciding on the width of the class intervals, you will have to find a compromise between having intervals short enough so that not all of the observations fall in the same interval, but long enough so that you do not end up with only one observation per interval.

It is also important to make sure that the class intervals are mutually exclusive.

Example 3 – Constructing a Frequency Distribution Table for Large Numbers of Observations

Thirty AA batteries were tested to determine how long they

would last. The results, to the nearest minute, were recorded as follows:

423, 369, 387, 411, 393, 394, 371, 377, 389, 409, 392, 408, 431, 401, 363, 391, 405, 382, 400, 381, 399, 415, 428, 422, 396, 372, 410, 419, 386, 390

Use the steps in previous examples and the above rules to help you construct a frequency distribution table.

Answer

The lowest value is 363 and the highest is 431.

Using the given data and a class interval of 10, the interval for the first class is 360 to 369 and includes 363 (the lowest value). Remember, there should always be enough class intervals so that the highest value is included.

The completed frequency distribution table should look like this:

Table 1. Life of AA batteries, in minutes

Battery life, minutes (x)	Tally	Frequency (f)
360–369	2	2
370–379	3	3
380–389	5	5
390–399	7	7
400–409	5	5
410–419	4	4
420–429	3	3
430–439	1	1
Total		**30**

Relative Frequency and Percentage Frequency

An analyst studying these data might want to know not only how long batteries last, but also what proportion of the batteries falls into each class interval of battery life.

This relative frequency of a particular observation or class interval is found by dividing the frequency (f) by the number of observations (n): that is, (f ÷ n). Thus:

Relative frequency = frequency ÷ number of observations

The percentage frequency is found by multiplying each relative frequency value by 100. Thus:

Percentage frequency = relative frequency × 100 = f ÷ n × 100

Continuous Data

Continuous data are numerical data that can theoretically be measured in infinitely small units. In other words, a continuous variable is one that, at least, theoretically can take any value between two points on a scale. Such variable can be measured with varying degrees of exactness depending on the measuring instrument. For example, weight, height, distance, time, percentage body fat, haemoglobin level, blood pressure, running speed, etc. can be measured to exact degrees up to any fractions. Data emerging from the measurement of these variables is continuous. The limit of a score in continuous variable may extend below and above the exact point to any fraction. Sometimes continuous data are given discrete values at certain thresholds, for example age a last birthday is a discrete value but age itself is a continuous quantity; in these situations it is reasonable to treat discrete values as continuous. Remember that information is lost when continuous data are recorded only in ranges (ordered categories), and the statistical analysis of continuous data is more powerful than that of categorical data.

Generally, in social sciences, continuous data are rarely used because of certain problems in measuring variables on continuous scales. Most variables are given discrete values. In order to interpret such values, account is taken of the mathematical true limits of a number. In general, true limits of a number are said to extend one half of a unit below and one half of a unit above that number and any score within those limits is rounded off to that number. Hence 81 pounds of body weight may be written either as 80.5 or 81.5 as its limits extend from 0.5 below to 0.5 above the actual measured value of this score.

Percentages or ratios summarise two pieces of information, namely their constituent numerator and denominator values. Simple ratios (0 to 1, i.e. the denominator is the maximum possible value that the numerator can take) can be treated as continuous data. More difficult to analyse data arise when the ratio represents a change, and the value can be negative. Ratios of observations compared with reference values, e.g. height relative to the mean of a reference population for a given sex and age, are difficult to handle as values may fall either side of 1 (100%).

Discrete Data

Dichotomous data emanates from the measurement of a discrete variable, which reflects the two mutually exclusive or contradictory categories (like when you flip a coin). Discrete data arise from observations that can only take certain numerical values, usually counts such as number of children or number of patients attending a clinic in a year. Other instances of this type of data include scores recorded as pass/fail, success/failure, true/false, yes/no, married/single, white/coloured, etc. Facts recorded this way cannot be subjected to any further division. However, it is possible in many instances to change dichotomous data into continuous data. Data may apply to present form or status of people rather than show their potential possibilities or refinement in their qualities. It is a matter of degree of refinement from the categorical to continuous. It is difficult, however, to distinguish the point when categorical data get transformed into continuous data. Precisely, a discrete variable is a variable which can take on numerical values that are specific distinct points on a scale such as members of a family, number of players in an athletic team or soldiers in a company. In discrete data the gap between scores - whether preceding or succeeding - is real and unbridgeable. For instance, there are only 11 players in a hockey team on the field at any moment, they cannot be eleven and half; there are only 40 desks in 6th class, it cannot 40½ nor 39½. Same way, sex or gender of people's is either male or female, there is nothing in between. In discrete data, fractional divisibility is neither possible nor acceptable. Discrete data may be treated as ordered categorical data in statistical analysis, but some information is lost in doing so.

CLASS DISTRIBUTION

Statistics is a very useful subject that is originated from mathematics. Its study is started in middle school and becomes a separate subject in higher-level mathematics. Statistics is a systematic study of collection, organization and analysis of data for a research or a survey. It is quite helpful in the forecast and prediction of various results from the well-organized data.

A statistical data may consists of a list of numbers related to a research. Among those numbers, few may be repeated twice and even more than twice. The repetition of number is a data set is termed as frequency of that particular number or the variable in which that number is assigned. The frequencies of variables in a data are to be listed in a table. This table is known as frequency distribution table and the list is referred as frequency distribution.

This page includes the study of frequency distribution with various examples. Our study on frequency distribution includes a study on cumulative frequency, mean frequency table. Frequency distribution can be defined as the tabulation of the values with one or more variables. A frequency distribution is defined as an orderly arrangement of data classified according to the magnitude of the observations.

There are many types of frequency distributions:

- Grouped frequency distribution
- Ungrouped frequency distribution
- Cumulative frequency distribution
- Relative frequency distribution
- Relative cumulative frequency distribution

FREQUENCY DISTRIBUTION?

A frequency distribution is an orderly arrangement of data classified according to the magnitude of the observations. When the data are grouped into classes of appropriate size indicating the number of observations in each class we get a frequency distribution. By forming frequency distribution, we can summarize the data effectively. It is a method of presenting the data in a summarized form. Frequency distribution is also known as Frequency table.

Uses of Frequency Distribution

1. Frequency distribution helps us to analyze the data.

2. Frequency distribution helps us to estimate the frequencies of the population on the basis of the ample.

3. Frequency distribution helps us to facilitate the computation

of various statistical measures.

FREQUENCY DISTRIBUTION TABLE

Frequency distribution table (also known as frequency table) consists of various components.

Classes: A large number of observations varying in a wide range are usually classified in several groups according to the size of their values. Each of these groups is defined by an interval called class interval. The class interval between 10 and 20 is defined as 10-20.

Class limits: The smallest and largest possible values in each class of a frequency distribution table are known as class limits. For the class 10-20, the class limits are 10 and 20. 10 is called the lower class limit and 20 is called the upper class limit.

Class limit: Class limit is the midmost value of the class interval. It is also known as the mid value.

Mid value of each class

$$= \frac{(\text{lower limit} + \text{Upper limit})}{2}$$

$$\frac{(0+10)}{2} = \frac{10}{2} = 5.$$

Magnitude of a class interval: The difference between the upper and lower limit of a class is called the magnitude of a class interval.

Class frequency: The number of observation falling within a class interval is called class frequency of that class interval.

Construct a Frequency Distribution

A frequency distribution table is one way to organize data so that it makes more sense. The data so distributed is called frequency distribution and the tabular form is called frequency distribution table. Let us see with the help of example how to construct distribution table.

The frequency distribution table lists all the marks and also show how many times (frequency) they occurred.

Number of marks	Tally marks	Frequency
1	~~||||~~ ||	7
2	~~||||~~	5
3	~~||||~~ |	6
4	~~||||~~	5
5	|||	3
Total		**26**

The number which tells us how many times a particular data appears is called the frequency. For example, 2 marks have been scored by five students which means marks 2 occurs five times. Therefore, the frequency of score 2 is five. Similarly, the frequency of marks 5 is three because three students scored five marks.

CONSTRUCTION OF TABLES

A statistical table has at least four major parts and some other minor parts.

(1) The Title

(2) The Box Head (column captions)

(3) The Stub (row captions)

(4) The Body

(5) Prefatory Notes

(6) Foots Notes

(7) Source Notes

The general sketch of table indicating its necessary parts is shown below:

-----THE TITLE----

----Prefatory Notes----

	----Box Head----
----Row Captions----	------Column Captions-----
---Stub Entries---	-----The Body-----

Foot Notes...

Source Notes...

(1) The Title:

A title is the main heading written in capital shown at the top of the table. It must explain the contents of the table and throw light on the table as whole different parts of the heading can be separated by commas there are no full stop be used in the little.

(2) The Box Head (column captions):

The vertical heading and subheading of the column are called columns captions. The spaces were these column headings are written is called box head. Only the first letter of the box head is in capital letters and the remaining words must be written in small letters.

(3) The Stub (row captions):

The horizontal headings and sub heading of the row are called row captions and the space where these rows headings are written is called stub.

(4) The Body:

It is the main part of the table which contains the numerical information classified with respect to row and column captions.

(5) Prefatory Notes :

A statement given below the title and enclosed in brackets usually describe the units of measurement is called prefatory notes.

(6) Foot Notes:

It appears immediately below the body of the table providing the further additional explanation.

(7) Source Notes:

The source notes is given at the end of the table indicating the source from when information has been taken. It includes the information about compiling agency, publication etc...

General Rules of Tabulation:

A table should be simple and attractive. There should be no need of further explanations (details).

Proper and clear headings for columns and rows should be need.

Suitable approximation may be adopted and figures may be rounded off.

The unit of measurement should be well defined.

If the observations are large in number they can be broken into two or three tables.

Thick lines should be used to separate the data under big classes and thin lines to separate the sub classes of data

13

Graphical Presentation of Class Distribution: Histogram, Frequency Polygon, Frequency Curve, Cumulative Frequency Polygon, Ogive and Pie Diagram

The statistical data may be presented in a more attractive form appealing to the eye with the helo of some graphic aids, i.e., pictures and graphs. Such presentation carries a lot of communication power. A mere glimpse of three picture and graphs may enable the viewer to have an immediate and meaningful grasp of the large amount of data.

Ungrouped data may be represented through a bar diagram, pie, diagram, pictograph and line graph. A graph can be said to be a mathematical picture. It provides a way of analyzing the problem in visual terms. Many problems can be reduced to visual form and such reduction often facilitates their understanding and solution. Although graphic representation has many forms, we shall discuss in this chapter only those forms which are useful in visualizing the important properties of frequency distributions and facilitate comparison of two or more frequency distributions. Since with the availability of latest computer software packages many variations could be made in graphical display, it is recommended that the students must understand the concepts discussed in this chapter in explaining various graphical design. Before discussing the method of constructing various types of graphs, we shall explain the general guidelines common to all kinds of graphical display of data.

HISTOGRAM

A histogram is a graphical representation of the distribution of numerical data. It is an estimate of the probability distribution of a continuous variable (quantitative variable) and was first introduced by Karl Pearson.

To construct a histogram, the first step is to "bin" the range of values—that is, divide the entire range of values into a series of intervals—and then count how many values fall into each interval. The bins are usually specified as consecutive, non-overlapping intervals of a variable. The bins (intervals) must be adjacent, and are often (but are not required to be) of equal size.

If the bins are of equal size, a rectangle is erected over the bin with height proportional to the frequency — the number of cases in each bin. A histogram may also be normalized to display "relative" frequencies. It then shows the proportion of cases that fall into each of several categories, with the sum of the heights equaling .

However, bins need not be of equal width; in that case, the erected rectangle is defined to have its area proportional to the frequency of cases in the bin. The vertical axis is then not the frequency but frequency density — the number of cases per unit of the variable on the horizontal axis.

As the adjacent bins leave no gaps, the rectangles of a histogram touch each other to indicate that the original variable is continuous.

Histograms give a rough sense of the density of the underlying distribution of the data, and often for density estimation: estimating the probability density function of the underlying variable. The total area of a histogram used for probability density is always normalized to 1. If the length of the intervals on the x-axis are all 1, then a histogram is identical to a relative frequency plot.

A histogram can be thought of as a simplistic kernel density estimation, which uses a kernel to smooth frequencies over the bins. This yields a smoother probability density function, which will in general more accurately reflect distribution of the underlying variable. The density estimate could be plotted as an alternative to the histogram, and is usually drawn as a curve rather than a set of boxes.

Another alternative is the average shifted histogram, which is fast to compute and gives a smooth curve estimate of the density without using kernels.

The histogram is one of the seven basic tools of quality control.

Histograms are sometimes confused with bar charts. A histogram is used for continuous data, where the bins represent ranges of data, while a bar chart is a plot of categorical variables. Some authors recommend that bar charts have gaps between the rectangles to clarify the distinction.

Consider the data in Table 1 on which histogram has been prepared in Figure 1 by using the guidelines discussed in the above section.

Table 1: *Frequency distribution of physical fitness scores for sample of 50 college students*

Class intervals	*Mid* x	*Lowest limit* f	*Frequency frequency*	*Cummu-lative*
1-10	5.5	0.5	2	2
11-20	15.5	10.5	7	9
21-30	25.5	20.5	5	14
31-40	35.5	30.5	5	19
41-50	45.5	40.5	9	28
51-60	55.5	50.5	8	36
61-70	65.5	60.5	6	42
71-80	75.5	70.5	5	47
81-90	85.5	80.5	2	49
91-100	95.5	90.5	1	50

Figure 1: *Histogram for the data on physical fitness for 50 students*

Here the upper limit of the class interval is considered to be the same as the lower limit of the next higher class interval for plotting the histogram.

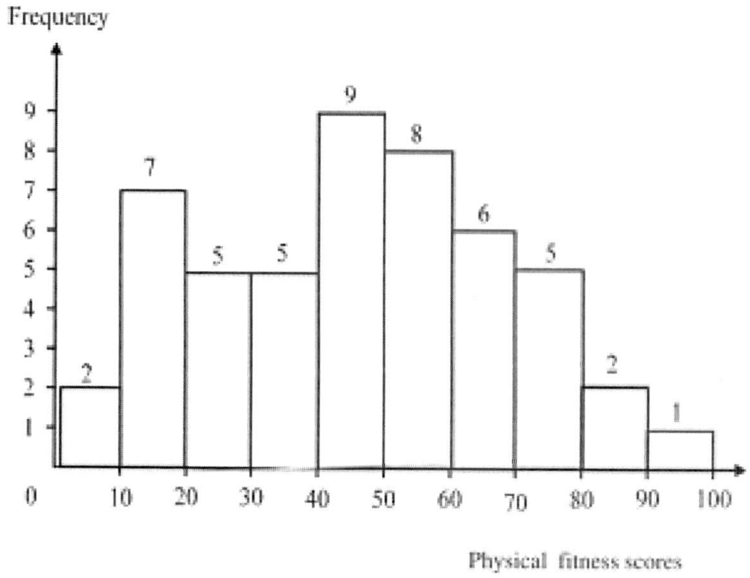

FREQUENCY POLYGON

A frequency polygon is very similar to a histogram. In fact, they are almost identical except that frequency polygons can be used to compare sets of data or to display a cumulative frequency distribution. In addition, histograms tend to be rectangles while a frequency polygon resembles a line graph.

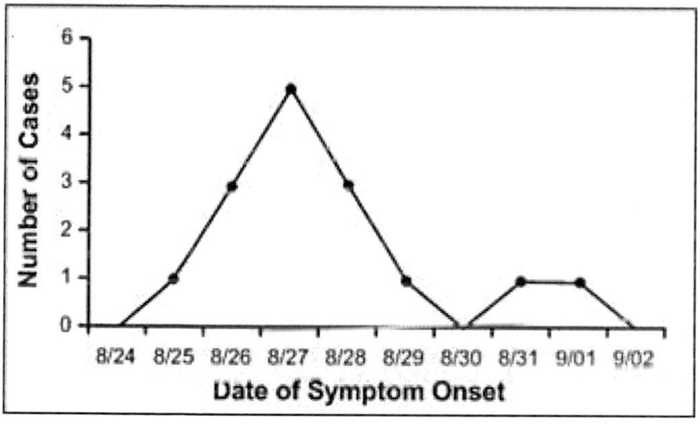

Fig. Number of Cases of Botulism by Date of Onset of Symptoms, Texas Church Supper Outbreak, 2001

The following data was used to graph the above frequency polygon. Dates with number of cases:

8/25:1

8/26:3

8/27:5

8/28:3

8/29:1

8/30:0

8/31:1

9/01:1

Step 1: Choose a bin size (class interval). See: What is a bin in statistics? For this frequency polygon, the CDC chose to organize bins by dates (8/25-9/01) with one date in each interval.

Step 2: Draw an x-axis to represent the data values. The x-axis for this chart is labeled "Date of symptom Onset."

Step 3: Place a tick mark in the center of each bin and label each bin with the middle value for the bin. Tick marks are usual, but this frequency polygon does not use them. However, the values (the dates in this case) are in the center of the bins.

Step 4: Draw a y-axis and mark the frequency of each bin with a single dot at the corresponding height.

Step 5: Connect the dots from left to right.

Tip: Convention is that you include one bin below your lowest value and one bin above your highest value. Notice that there are two intervals (i.e. two dates) either side of the first and last case where there are no cases. The graph touches the x-axis at these points.

Frequency polygons are a graphical device for understanding the shapes of distributions. They serve the same purpose as histograms, but are especially helpful for comparing sets of data. Frequency polygons are also a good choice for displaying cumulative frequency distributions.

To create a frequency polygon, start just as for histograms, by choosing a class interval. Then draw an X-axis representing the values of the scores in your data. Mark the middle of each class interval with a tick mark, and label it with the middle value represented by the class. Draw the Y-axis to indicate the frequency of each class. Place a point in the middle of each class interval at the height corresponding to its frequency. Finally, connect the points. You should include one class interval below the lowest value in your data and one above the highest value. The graph will then touch the X-axis on both sides.

A frequency polygon for 642 psychology test scores shown in Figure 1 was constructed from the frequency table shown in Table 1.

Table 1. Frequency Distribution of Psychology Test Scores

Lower Limit	Upper Limit	Count	Cumulative Count
29.5	39.5	0	0
39.5	49.5	3	3
49.5	59.5	10	13
59.5	69.5	53	66
69.5	79.5	107	173
79.5	89.5	147	320
89.5	99.5	130	450
99.5	109.5	78	528
109.5	119.5	59	587
119.5	129.5	36	623
129.5	139.5	11	634
139.5	149.5	6	640
149.5	159.5	1	641
159.5	169.5	1	642
169.5	179.5	0	642

The first label on the X-axis is 35. This represents an interval extending from 29.5 to 39.5. Since the lowest test score is 46, this interval has a frequency of 0. The point labeled 45 represents the interval from 39.5 to 49.5. There are three scores in this interval. There are 147 scores in the interval that surrounds 85.

You can easily discern the shape of the distribution from Figure 1. Most of the scores are between 65 and 115. It is clear that the distribution is not symmetric inasmuch as good scores (to the right) trail off more gradually than poor scores (to the left). In the terminology of Chapter 3 (where we will study shapes of distributions more systematically), the distribution is skewed.

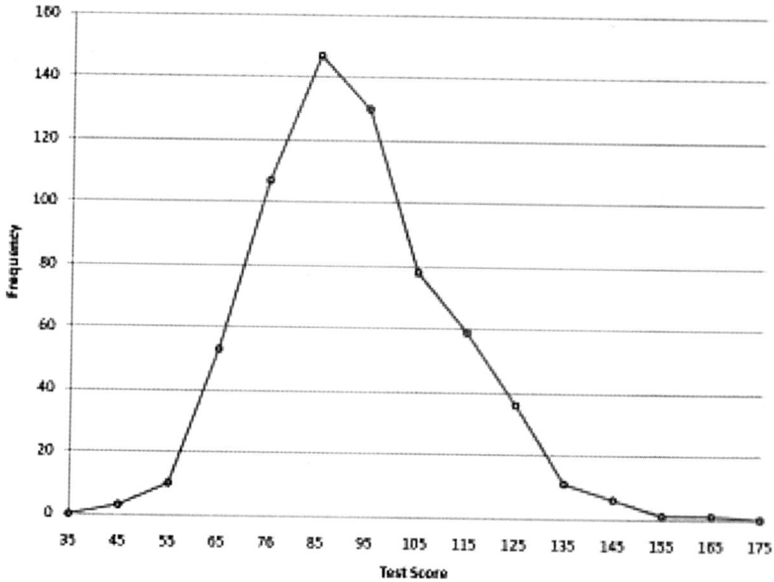

Figure 1. Frequency polygon for the psychology test scores

A cumulative frequency polygon for the same test scores is shown in Figure 2. The graph is the same as before except that the Y value for each point is the number of students in the corresponding class interval plus all numbers in lower intervals. For example, there are no scores in the interval labeled "35," three in the interval "45," and 10 in the interval "55." Therefore, the Y value corresponding to "55" is 13. Since 642 students took the test, the cumulative frequency for the last interval is 642.

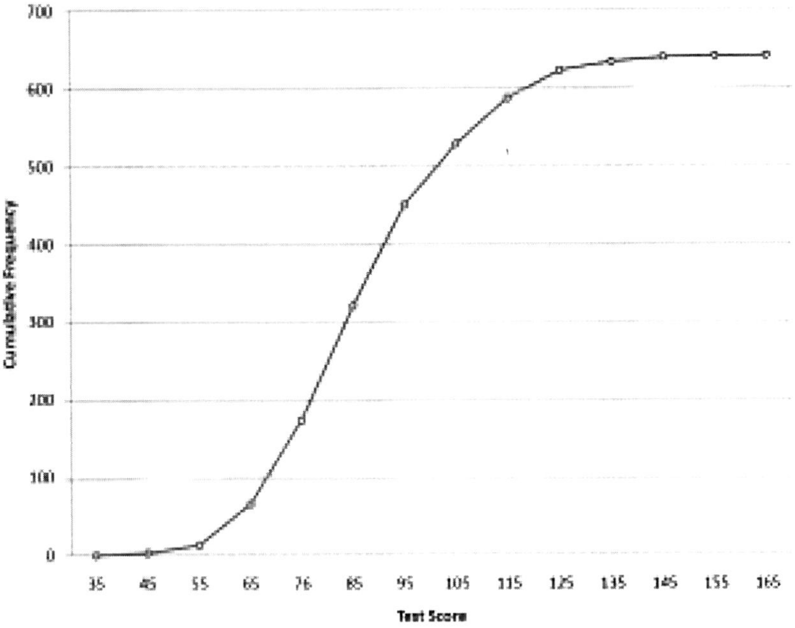

Figure 2. Cumulative frequency polygon for the psychology test scores

Frequency polygons are useful for comparing distributions. This is achieved by overlaying the frequency polygons drawn for different data sets. Figure 3 provides an example. The data come from a task in which the goal is to move a computer cursor to a target on the screen as fast as possible. On 20 of the trials, the target was a small rectangle; on the other 20, the target was a large rectangle. Time to reach the target was recorded on each trial. The two distributions (one for each target) are plotted together in Figure 3. The figure shows that, although there is some overlap in times, it generally took longer to move the cursor to the small target than to the large one.

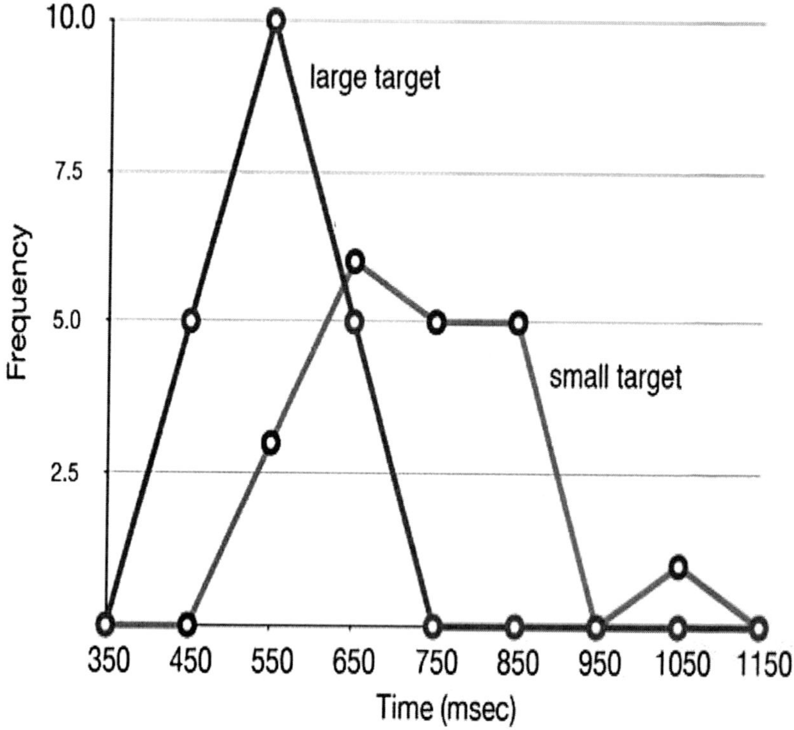

Figure 3. Overlaid frequency polygons.

It is also possible to plot two cumulative frequency distributions in the same graph. This is illustrated in Figure 4 using the same data from the cursor task. The difference in distributions for the two targets is again evident.

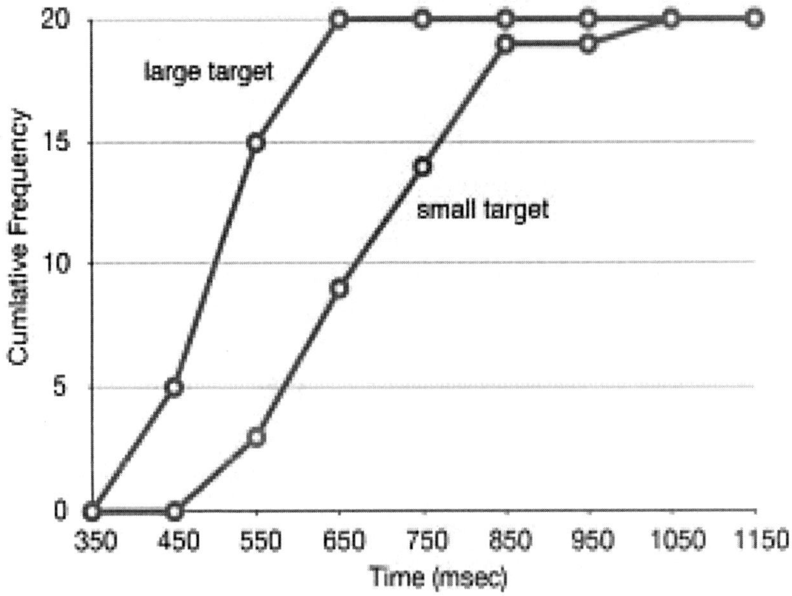

Figure 4. Overlaid cumulative frequency polygons

FREQUENCY CURVE

Frequency Curve is a smooth curve which corresponds to the limiting case of a histogram computed for a frequency distribution of a continuous distribution as the number of data points becomes very large.

Frequency Curve is obtained by joining the points of frequency polygon by a freehand smoothed curve. Unlike frequency polygon, where the points we joined by straight lines, we make use of free hand joining of those points in order to get a smoothed frequency curve. It is used to remove the ruggedness of polygon and to present it in a good form or shape. We smoothen the angularities of the polygon only without making any basic change in the shape of the curve. In this case also the curve begins and ends at base line, as is in case of polygon. Area under the curve must remain almost the same as in the case of polygon.

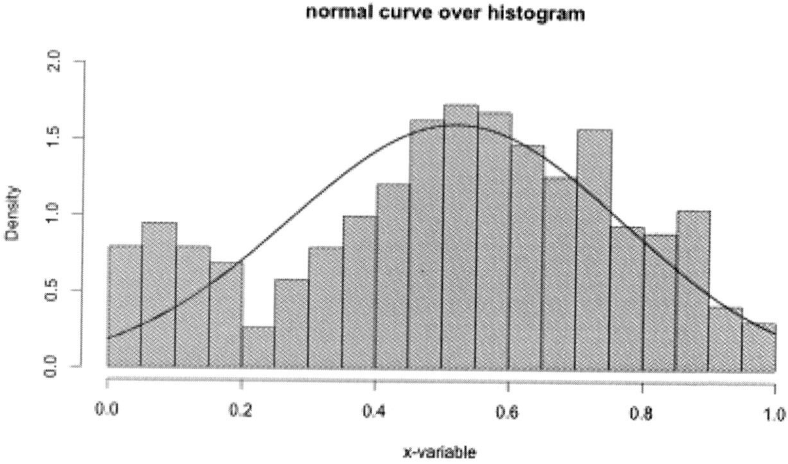

CUMULATIVE FREQUENCY POLYGON

A cumulative frequency polygon is a plot of the cumulative frequency against the upper class boundary with the points joined by a line segment. An ogive is any continuous cumulative frequency curve, including cumulative frequency polygons. A cumulative frequency polygon displays cumulative frequency on the x-axis and class marks on the y-axis.

Frequency polygons are line graphs joined by all the midpoints at the top of the bars of histograms. Frequency polygons illustrate the shape of the distribution of the data. The endpoints of a frequency polygon lie on the x-axis. To construct a frequency polygon, a bar graph or histogram must first be drawn. Then, a line graph is drawn over the bar graph. Frequency polygons and histograms are similar in that they show the same information but in a different manner. When comparing two different sets of data, it is often easier to display the data using a frequency polygon versus a histogram. Some examples of data illustrated in a frequency polygon are the number of vehicles passing through a particular point in a route, the number of hours a student in a class spends studying and the display of exam scores between two different sets of students.

A frequency polygon whose vertices represent the sum of all previous class frequencies of the data. For example, if a frequency polygon had vertices of 5, 8, 3, 7, and 10, the cumulative frequency polygon on the same data would have vertices of 5, 13, 16, 23, and 33. As another example, a cumulative frequency distribution for scores on a psychology test is shown below.

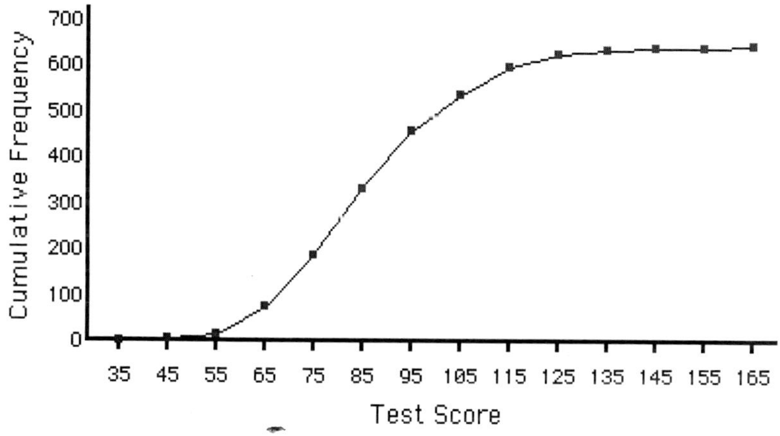

OGIVE

In statistics, an ogive is a free-hand graph showing the curve of a cumulative distribution function. The points plotted are the upper class limit and the corresponding cumulative frequency. (which, for the normal distribution, resembles one side of an Arabesque or ogival arch).

An ogive (oh-jive), sometimes called a cumulative frequency polygon, is a type of frequency polygon that shows cumulative frequencies. In other words, the cumulative percents are added on the graph from left to right.

A plot of the cumulative frequency against the upper class boundary with the points joined by line segments. Any continuous cumulative frequency curve, including a cumulative frequency polygon, is called an "Ogive".

Example question: Draw an Ogive graph for the following set of data:

02, 07, 16, 21, 31, 03, 08, 17, 21, 55

03, 13, 18, 22, 55, 04, 14, 19, 25, 57

06, 15, 20, 29, 58.

Step 1: Make a relative frequency table from the data. The first column has the class limits, the second column has the frequency (the count) and the third column has the relative frequency (class frequency / total number of items):

Class Limits	Frequency	Relative Frequency (#/Total)
01 to 09	5	5/25 = .20
10 to 19	5	5/25 = .20
20 to 29	6	6/25 = 0.24
30 to 39	1	1/25 = 0.04
40 to 49	0	0/25 = 0
50 to 59	8	8/25 = 0.32

If you aren't sure how to create your class limits(also called bins), watch the video at the bottom of this article or see: What is a Bin in Statistics?

Step 2: Add a fourth column and cumulate (add up) the frequencies in column 2, going down from top to bottom. For example, the second entry is the sum of the first row and the second row in the frequency column (5 + 5 = 10), and the third entry is the sum of the first, second, and third rows in the frequency column (5 + 5 + 6 = 16):

Class Limits	Frequency	Relative Frequency (#/Total)	Cumulative Frequency
01 to 09	5	5/25 = 20	5
10 to 19	5	5/25 = .20	10
20 to 29	6	6/25 = 0.24	16
30 to 39	1	1/25 = 0.04	17
40 to 49	0	0/25 = 0	17
50 to 59	8	8/25 = 0.32	25

Step 3: Add a fifth column and cumulate the relative frequencies from column 3. If you do this step correctly, your values should add up to 100% (or 1 as a decimal):

Class Limits	Frequency	Relative Frequency (#/Total)	Cumulative Frequency	Cumulative Rel. Freq.
01 to 09	5	5/25 = 20	5	0.2
10 to 19	5	5/25 = .20	10	0.4
20 to 29	6	6/25 = 0.24	16	0.64
30 to 39	1	1/25 = 0.04	17	0.68
40 to 49	0	0/25=0	17	0.68
50 to 59	8	8/25 = 0.32	25	1

Step 4: Draw an x-y graph with percent cumulative relative frequency on the y-axis (from 0 to 100%, or as a decimal, 0 to 1). Mark the x-axis with the class boundaries.

Step 5: Plot your points. Note: Each point should be plotted on the upper limit of the class boundary. For example, if your first class boundary is 0 to 10, the point should be plotted at 10.

Step 6: Connect the dots with straight lines. the ogive is one continuous line, made up of several smaller lines that connect pairs of dots, moving from left to right.

The finished graph for this sample data:

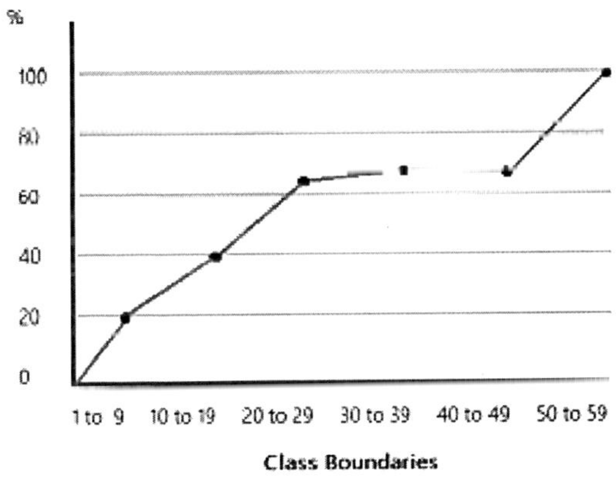

PIE DIAGRAM

A pie chart (or a circle chart) is a circular statistical graphic which is divided into slices to illustrate numerical proportion. In a pie chart, the arc length of each slice (and consequently its central angle and area), is proportional to the quantity it represents. While it is named for its resemblance to a pie which has been sliced, there are variations on the way it can be presented. The earliest known pie chart is generally credited to William Playfair's Statistical Breviary of 1801.

Pie charts are very widely used in the business world and the mass media. However, they have been criticized, and many experts recommend avoiding them, pointing out that research has shown it is difficult to compare different sections of a given pie chart, or to compare data across different pie charts. Pie charts can be replaced in most cases by other plots such as the bar chart, box plot or dot plots.

History

The earliest known pie chart is generally credited to William Playfair's Statistical Breviary of 1801, in which two such graphs are used. Playfair presented an illustration, which contained a series of pie charts. One of those charts depicting the proportions of the Turkish Empire located in Asia, Europe and Africa before 1789. This invention was not widely used at first;

The French engineer Charles Joseph Minard was one of the first to use pie charts in 1858, in particular in maps. Minard's map, 1858 used pie charts to represent the cattle sent from all around France for consumption in Paris (1858).

Playfair thought that pie charts were in need of a third dimension to add additional information. It has been said that Florence Nightingale invented it, though in fact she just popularised it and she was later assumed to have created it due to the obscurity of Playfair's creation

VARIANTS AND SIMILAR CHARTS

3d Pie Cake/Perspective Pie Cake

A 3d pie cake, or perspective pie cake, is used to give the chart a 3D look. Often used for aesthetic reasons, the third dimension does not improve the reading of the data; on the contrary, these plots are difficult to interpret because of the distorted effect of perspective associated with the third dimension. The use of superfluous dimensions not used to display the data of interest is discouraged for charts in general, not only for pie charts.

Doughnut Chart

A doughnut chart (also spelled donut) is a variant of the pie chart, with a blank center allowing for additional information about the data as a whole to be included.

Exploded Pie Chart

A chart with one or more sectors separated from the rest of the disk is known as an exploded pie chart. This effect is used to either highlight a sector, or to highlight smaller segments of the chart with small proportions.

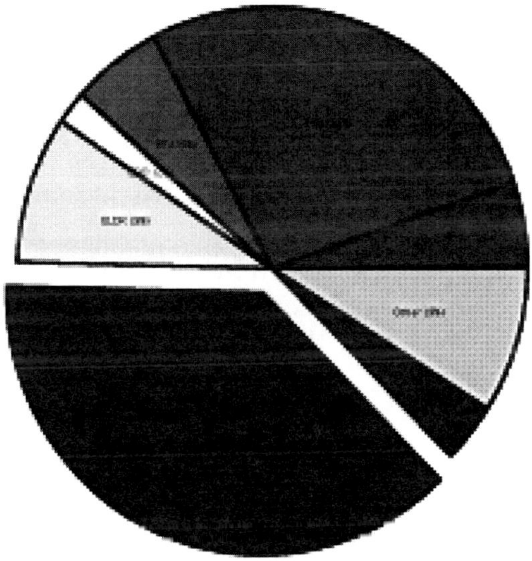

Polar Area Diagram

The polar area diagram is similar to a usual pie chart, except sectors are equal angles and differ rather in how far each sector extends from the center of the circle. The polar area diagram is used to plot cyclic phenomena (e.g., count of deaths by month). For example, if the count of deaths in each month for a year are to be plotted then there will be 12 sectors (one per month) all with the same angle of 30 degrees each. The radius of each sector would be proportional to the square root of the death count for the month, so the area of a sector represents the number of deaths in a month. If the death count in each month is subdivided by cause of death, it is possible to make multiple comparisons on one diagram, as is seen in the polar area diagram famously developed by Florence Nightingale.

The first known use of polar area diagrams was by André-Michel Guerry, which he called courbes circulaires, in an 1829 paper showing seasonal and daily variation in wind direction over the year and births and deaths by hour of the day. Léon Lalanne later used a polar diagram to show the frequency of wind directions around compass points in 1843. The wind rose is still used by meteorologists. Nightingale published her rose diagram in 1858. The name "coxcomb" is sometimes used erroneously: this was the name Nightingale used to refer to a book containing the diagrams rather than the diagrams themselves.

Ring Chart / Sunburst Chart / Multilevel Pie Char

A ring chart, also known as a sunburst chart or a multilevel pie chart, is used to visualize hierarchical data, depicted by concentric circles. The circle in the centre represents the root node, with the hierarchy moving outward from the center. A segment of the inner circle bears a hierarchical relationship to those segments of the outer circle which lie within the angular sweep of the parent segment.

Spie Chart

A variant of the polar area chart is the spie chart designed by Dror Feitelson. This superimposes a normal pie chart with a modified polar area chart to permit the comparison of two sets of related data. The base pie chart represents the first data set in the usual way, with different slice sizes. The second set is represented by the superimposed polar area chart, using the same angles as the base, and adjusting the radii to fit the data. For example, the base pie chart could show the distribution of age and gender groups in a population, and the overlay their representation among road casualties. Age and gender groups that are especially susceptible to being involved in accidents then stand out as slices that extend

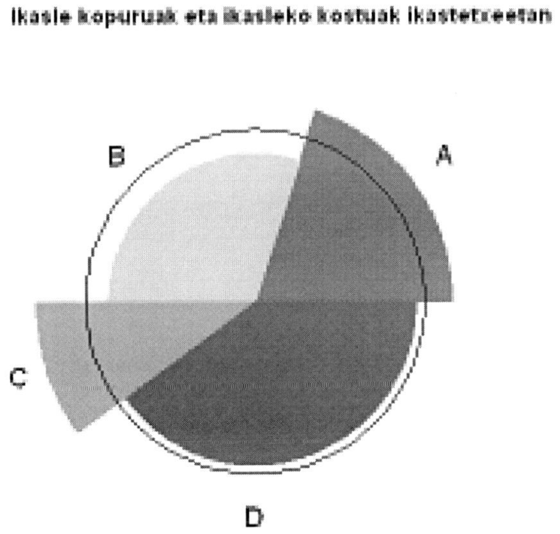

beyond the original pie chart.

Square Chart

Square charts are a rare form of pie charts that use squares instead of circles to represent percentages. Similar to basic circular pie charts, square pie charts take each percentage out of a total 100%

Example

The following example chart is based on preliminary results of the election for the European Parliament in 2004. The table lists the number of seats allocated to each party group, along with the derived percentage of the total that they each make up. The values in the last column, the derived central angle of each sector, Is found by multiplying the percentage by 360°.

Group	Seats	Percent (%)	Central angle (°)
EUL	39	5.3	19.2
PES	200	27.3	98.4
EFA	42	5.7	20.7
EDD	15	2.0	7.4
ELDR	67	9.2	33.0

(Contd. ...)

Group	Seats	Percent (%)	Central angle (°)
EPP	276	37.7	135.7
UEN	27	3.7	13.3
Other	66	9.0	32.5
Total	732	99.9*	360.2*

*Because of rounding, these totals do not add up to 100 and 360.

The size of each central angle is proportional to the size of the corresponding quantity, here the number of seats. Since the sum of the central angles has to be 360°, the central angle for a quantity that is a fraction Q of the total is 360Q degrees. In the example, the central angle for the largest group (European People's Party (EPP)) is 135.7° because 0.377 times 360, rounded to one decimal place, equals 135.7.

Use and Effectiveness

An obvious flaw exhibited by pie charts is that they cannot show more than a few values without separating the visual encoding (the "slices") from the data they represent (typically percentages). When slices become too small, pie charts have to rely on colors, textures or arrows so the reader can understand them. This makes them unsuitable for use with larger amounts of data. Pie charts also take up a larger amount of space on the page compared to the more flexible bar charts, which do not need to have separate legends, and can display other values such as averages or targets at the same time.

Statisticians generally regard pie charts as a poor method of displaying information, and they are uncommon in scientific literature. One reason is that it is more difficult for comparisons to be made between the size of items in a chart when area is used instead of length and when different items are shown as different shapes.

Further, in research performed at AT&T Bell Laboratories, it was shown that comparison by angle was less accurate than comparison by length. This can be illustrated with the adjacent

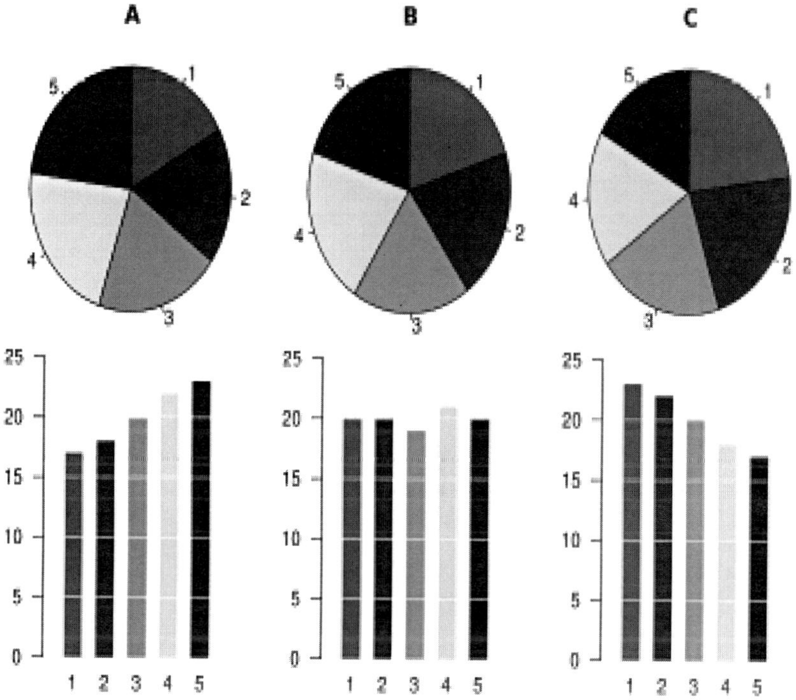

diagram, showing three pie charts, and, below each of them, the corresponding bar chart representing the same data. Most subjects have difficulty ordering the slices in the pie chart by size; when the bar chart is used the comparison is much easier. Similarly, comparisons between data sets are easier using the bar chart. However, if the goal is to compare a given category (a slice of the pie) with the total (the whole pie) in a single chart and the multiple is close to 25 or 50 percent, then a pie chart can often be more effective than a bar graph.

The example (left) is of a pie chart with 18 values, having to separate the data from its representation. Note also that several values are represented with the same color, making interpretation difficult.

Several studies presented at the European Visualization Conference analyzed the relative accuracy of several pie chart formats, reaching the conclusion that pie charts and doughnut

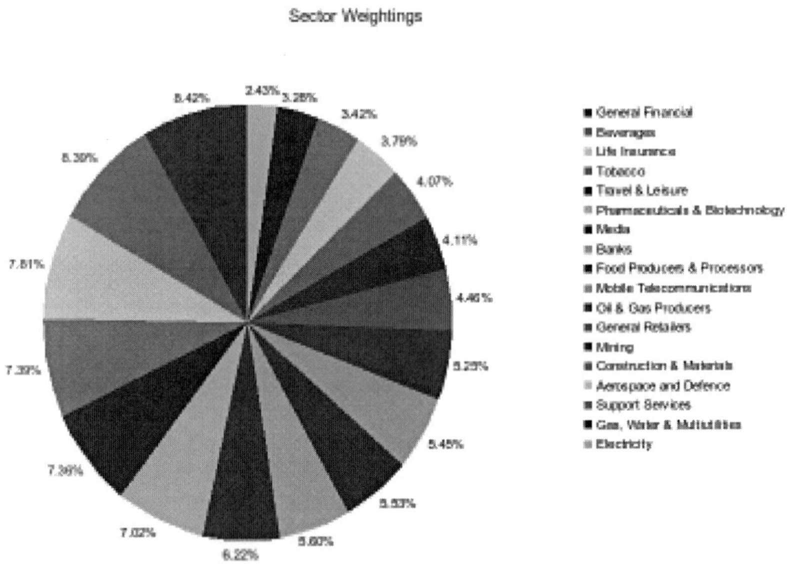

charts produce similar error levels when reading them, and square pie charts provide the most accurate reading

Selected References

Chatterji,Samprit, and Chaterji, Sangit. *New Lamps for Old: An Exploratory Analysis of Running Times in Olympic Games*, App. Statist., 1982, 31, 14-22.

Elandt-Johnson, Regina G. *Probability Models and Statistical Methods in Genetics*. New York: John Wiley & Sons, 1971.

Freund, J.E, Williams,F.J. and B.M. Perles, *Elementary Business Statistics*, 6th Ed., Engelwood Cliffs, NJ, Prentice Hall, 1993.

Kemeny, John G., and Snell, J. Laurie. *Mathematical Models in Social Sciences*. Boston: Ginn & Co., 1962.

McClave, J.T. and Benson, P.G., *Statistics for Business and Economics*, 6th ed., Engelwood Cliffs, NJ, Prentice Hall,1994.

Chambers, John M.; Cleveland, William S.; Kleiner, Beat; and Tukey, Paul A. *Graphical Methods for Data Analysis*, Belmont, Calif.: Wadsworth International Group, 1983.

Cleveland,W.S., *The Elements of Graphing Data*, rev.ed., Murray Hill, NJ, AT&T Bell Laboratories,1994.

Kapur, S.K. *Elements of Practical Statistics*. New Delhi: Oxford & IBH Publishing Co., 1981.

Tufte,E.R., *The Visual Display of Quantitative Information*, Chelshire,CT, Graphics Press, 1983.

Wallis, W.A., and Roberts, H.V. *Statistics: A New Approach. New York: The Free Press of Glencoe*, 1956.

Croxton, Frederick E., Cowden, Dudley J., and Klein, Sidney. *Applied General Statistics*. New Delhi: Prentice Hall of India, 1979.

Kurtz, Albert K., and Mayo, Samuel T. *Statistical Methods in Education and Psychology*. New Delhi: Narosa Publishing House, 1980.

Mendenhall,W., and Sincich,T., *A Second Course in Statistics: Regression Analysis*, 5th ed., Englewood Cliffs, NJ, Prentice Hall, 1996.

Verma, J.P., *A Textbook on Sports Statistics*, 2011, Sports Publication, New Delhi.

Buchha, Abhay N., *Management of Physical Education and Statistics*, 2009, Sports Publication, New Delhi.

Mishra, Srikantha, *Research and Statistics in Physical Education*, Sports Publication, New Delhi.

Kutty, S.K., *Research Methodology*, 2014, Sports Publication, New Delhi.

Shaw, Dhananjoy, *Fundamental Statistics in Physical Education and Sports Sciences*, 1998, Sports Publication, New Delhi.

UNIT- 4
Statistical Models in Physical Education and Sports

14
Measures of Central Tendency: Mean, Median and Mode—Meaning, Definition, Importance, Advantages, Disadvantages and Calculation from Group and Ungrouped Data

MEASURES OF CENTRAL TENDENCY

In statistics, a central tendency (or measure of central tendency) is a central or typical value for a probability distribution. It may also be called a center or location of the distribution. Colloquially, measures of central tendency are often called averages. The term central tendency dates from the late 1920s.

The most common measures of central tendency are the arithmetic mean, the median and the mode. A central tendency can be calculated for either a finite set of values or for a theoretical distribution, such as the normal distribution. Occasionally authors use central tendency to denote "the tendency of quantitative data to cluster around some central value."

The central tendency of a distribution is typically contrasted with its dispersion or variability; dispersion and central tendency are the often characterized properties of distributions. Analysts may judge whether data has a strong or a weak central tendency based on its dispersion.

Measures of Central Tendency

The following may be applied to one-dimensional data. Depending on the circumstances, it may be appropriate to transform the data before calculating a central tendency. Examples are squaring the values or taking logarithms. Whether a transformation is appropriate and what it should be, depend heavily on the data being analyzed.

- **Arithmetic mean (or simply, mean)** – the sum of all measurements divided by the number of observations in the data set.

- **Median** – the middle value that separates the higher half from the lower half of the data set. The median and the mode are the only measures of central tendency that can be used for ordinal data, in which values are ranked relative to each other but are not measured absolutely.

- **Mode** – the most frequent value in the data set. This is the only central tendency measure that can be used with nominal data, which have purely qualitative category assignments.

- **Geometric mean** – the nth root of the product of the data values, where there are n of these. This measure is valid only for data that are measured absolutely on a strictly positive scale.

- **Harmonic mean** – the reciprocal of the arithmetic mean of the reciprocals of the data values. This measure too is valid only for data that are measured absolutely on a strictly positive scale.

- **Weighted arithmetic mean** – an arithmetic mean that incorporates weighting to certain data elements.

- **Truncated mean (or trimmed mean)** – the arithmetic mean of data values after a certain number or proportion of the highest and lowest data values have been discarded.

- **Interquartile mean** – a truncated mean based on data within the interquartile range.

- **Midrange** – the arithmetic mean of the maximum and minimum values of a data set.

- **Midhinge** – the arithmetic mean of the two quartiles.

- **Trimean** – the weighted arithmetic mean of the median and two quartiles.

• **Winsorized mean** – an arithmetic mean in which extreme values are replaced by values closer to the median.

Any of the above may be applied to each dimension of multi-dimensional data, but the results may not be invariant to rotations of the multi-dimensional space. In addition, there is the

• **Geometric median** - which minimizes the sum of distances to the data points. This is the same as the median when applied to one-dimensional data, but it is not the same as taking the median of each dimension independently. It is not invariant to different rescaling of the different dimensions.

The Quadratic mean (often known as the root mean square) is useful in engineering, but is not often used in statistics. This is because it is not a good indicator of the center of the distribution when the distribution includes negative values.

Solutions to Variational Problems

Several measures of central tendency can be characterized as solving a variational problem, in the sense of the calculus of variations, namely minimizing variation from the center. That is, given a measure of statistical dispersion, one asks for a measure of central tendency that minimizes variation: such that variation from the center is minimal among all choices of center. In a quip, "dispersion precedes location". In the sense of L^p spaces, the correspondence is:

L^p	Dispersion	Central Tendency
L^1	Average absolute deviation	median
L^2	Standard deviation	mean
L^8	Maximum deviation	midrange

Thus standard deviation about the mean is lower than standard deviation about any other point, and the maximum deviation about the midrange is lower than the maximum deviation about any other point. The uniqueness of this characterization of mean follows from convex optimization. Indeed, for a given (fixed) data set x, the function represents the dispersion about a constant value c relative to the L^2 norm. Because the function f_2 is a strictly convex coercive function, the minimizer exists and is unique.

Note that the median in this sense is not in general unique, and in fact any point between the two central points of a discrete distribution minimizes average absolute deviation. The dispersion in the L1 norm, given by

$$f_1(c) = \|x - c\|_1$$

is not strictly convex, whereas strict convexity is needed to ensure uniqueness of the minimizer. In spite of this, the minimizer is unique for the L^8 norm.

Relationships Between the Mean, Median and Mode

For unimodal distributions the following bounds are known and are sharp:

$$\frac{|\theta - \mu|}{\sigma} \leq \sqrt{3},$$

$$\frac{|v - \mu|}{\sigma} \leq \sqrt{0.6},$$

$$\frac{|\theta - v|}{\sigma} \leq \sqrt{3},$$

where μ is the mean, v is the median, θ is the mode, and s is the standard deviation.

For every distribution

$$\frac{|v - \mu|}{\sigma} \leq \sqrt{1},$$

For every distribution

Measures of central tendency – *a fancy* name for mean, median and mode - are measures of the location of the middle or the centre of a distribution, and provide the very foundation of statistics. These three summarize an entire distribution of scores by describing the most typical score of the cases (the mean), the middle case (the median), or common score (the mode) of that distribution. These statistics are powerful because they can reduce huge arrays of data to a single, easily understood number.

Today, statistical procedures used in research are fully computerized. One data are fed into the computer, required statistical measures can be obtained in a matter of seconds depending upon the type software used. However, it is good for the researchers to calculate simple statistical measures manually which helps them understand their meanings and application fully and more productively. Calculation of various elementary statistics is explained hereunder for researchers' benefit.

THE MEAN

By definition, mean is *a point along the continuum of a given set of scores, the sum of scores above which and below which is equal in magnitude.* Also known as arithmetic mean, it is the most commonly used measure of central tendency, and is the score that is located at the precise mathematical centre of the distribution. Mean is calculated by adding together all the scores in a group, and then divide the sum of scores by the total number of items (scores) in the group. Mean has several properties: (1) it is the most reliable and most often used measure of central tendency; (2) it need not be an actual score in the distribution; (3) it is strongly influenced by outliers (extreme scores); and (4) the sum of the deviations about the mean must always equal zero. An outlier is a score that lies apart from most of the rest of the distribution. If there are several outliers in a distribution it will often result in skewed shape to the distribution. Outliers tend to pull central tendency measures with them. The use of mean is only justified when the researcher is dealing with the interval-ratio data.

For the mean, the formula in summation notation is:

m = SX/N where m is the ***population mean*** and N is the number of scores.

If the scores are from a ***sample,*** then the symbol M refers to the mean and N refers to the sample size. The formula for M is the same as the formula for m.

$$M = SX/N$$

Characteristics of the Mean

- It is typically always the centre of (gravity of) any distribution of scores, and a point around which all of the scores cancel out S(Xi-M) = 0. This algebraic relationship between the scores and the mean indicates that the mean is a good descriptive measure of the centrality of scores.

- The mean is relatively reliable in the sense that it does not vary too much when repeated samples are taken from the same population at least not as much as some other kind of statistical descriptions.
- Being determined by a rigid formula, it lends itself to subsequent algebraic treatment better than the other two measures, i.e. median and mode.
- S(Xi-M) = minimum. If the differences between the scores and the mean are squared and then added, the resultant sum will be less than the sum of the squared differences between the scores and any other point in the distribution.
- Every score in the distribution affects the mean. The mode and median are not so affected. This quality is both an advantage and a disadvantage. The mean utilizes all the available information—each score in the distribution influences the mean. On the other hand, when a distribution has a few extreme cases (very high or very low scores), the mean may become very misleading as a measure of centrality.

(A) CALCULATING THE MEAN FROM UNGROUPED DATA

Table 1: Scores of Cyclists on Pull Ups

Athlete	Score (X)	Distance from the Mean
	Paul 10	+ 3.2
John	9	+ 2.2
Mohinder	8	+ 1.2 = + 6.6
Pappa	5	– 1.8
Timmy	2	– 4.8 = – 6.6
N = 5	Total = 34	

(It is the central value of the distribution and is not accredited to any one player. It is, therefore, a typical performance of the group as a whole).

Statistical symbols used decoded

X = Mean S = "Sum of " X = Scores

N= Number of Cases

(B) CALCULATING THE MEAN FROM GROUPED DATA

When cases are large, the mean is calculated by arranging the raw data into a frequency table as explained above (Table 2). The score of twenty female basketball players on a test of intelligence are transformed into a frequency Table (Table 4) by following the procedure enumerated in Table 2.

Table 2: Female Basketball Players' Intelligence Scores (N=20)

Step Interval	*Midpoint (X)*	*Frequency (f)*	*FX*
30-34	32	2	64
25-29	27	2	54
20-24	22	6	110
15-19	17	6	102
10-14	12	4	48
5-9	7	1	7
		N = 20	SFX=385

Mean = S FX/N
= 385/20
= 19.25

THE MEDIAN

The median is defined *as that point on the continuum of scores above which and below which fall the 50% of the measures.* It is the physical centre of the distribution. If scores were ordered from the lowest to the highest, the median would be the score right in the middle; in other words, it is the value in the middle when the values of the distribution are sequentially arranged. The median is resistant to outliers (the extreme scores). That is, outliers will generally not affect the median and it will not be affected as much as the mean.

(a) Calculating Median from an Ungrouped Data

When the data are ungrouped, the median will be calculated by first arranging the data in rank order according the magnitude, and then locating the midpoint at first sight by applying the following formula :

$$\text{Median} = \left(\frac{N+1}{2}\right) \text{ the measures in order of size}$$

For example, the distribution 1, 1, 2, 2, 3, (**4**), 5, 5, 5, 6, 7, with each figure placed in order of magnitude, has a median value of 4 because there are five values above this point and five values below this point. The median is easy to locate when the number of scores is odd as in this case but when there is an even set of numbers then there will be two values that are at the centre. These will summed up and averaged in order to determine the median. For example, if we take out one of the numbers in the distribution so that we have 1, 1, 2, 2, 3, 4, 5, 5, 5, 6 then the two values in the centre are 3 and 4 (1, 1, 2, 2, 3, 4, 5, 5, 5, 6). The average is **3.5** and that is the median.

(b) Calculating the Median from Grouped Data

When scores in a continuous series are grouped into a frequency distribution (as in table - 13.6), the median will be the 50% point in the said distribution, to be formally calculated by following the steps enumerated below:

(1) Divide the total number of scores by two i.e. N/2 one half of the cases in the distribution.

(2) Start at the low-end of the distribution and total up the frequencies placed against each interval until the lower limit of the interval containing the median is reached. The sum of these scores is F.

(3) Subtract the sum obtained in step 2 from the number necessary to reach the median i.e. $\frac{N}{2} - F$

(4) Now calculate the proportion of the median interval that must be added to its lower limit in order to reach the median score. This is done by dividing the number obtained in step 3 above by the number of scores (fm) in the median interval and then multiplying it by the size of the interval.

$$\frac{\frac{N}{2} - F}{fm}$$

(5) Add the amount obtained by the calculation made in step 4 above to the exact lower limit (step 1) which contains the median.

The brief of the steps 1-5 procedure above, is seen in the following formula:

$$Median = L + \frac{\left(\frac{N}{2} - F\right)}{fm} \times Si$$

Symbols used decoded

L = exact lower limit of the median interval

N = total number of scores

F = sum of the frequencies in the interval below L

fm = number of scores within the median interval

Si = step interval or class interval

THE MODE

The *most frequently occurring score* in a distribution is called the *mode,* technically referred to as crude mode. The crude mode is not normally applied to ungrouped data because any particular score might occur haphazardly at any point in a series of observations and be quite unrepresentative of the data as a whole. In the series of 3, 4, 4, 6, 7, 7, 7 and 8, 7 is the most occurring measure, hence its Crude Mode. When data are grouped, the modal score can hardly be identified because such a score is lost within a specific interval of the grouped distribution. However, it is not difficult to identify the Modal Class - the interval containing the maximum scores.

Occasionally, a distribution may have more than one mode. Such distributions are called bimodal having (two modes) or tri-modal (having three modes). When the mean and the median of a distribution are known, its mode can be calculated by the following formula.

Mode = (3 Median - 2 Mean)

ADVANTAGES AND DISADVANTAGES OF MEAN, MEDIAN AND MODE

MEAN

Advantages of Arithemetic Mean

The arithmetic mean (or simply "mean") of a sample is the sum of the sampled values divided by the number of items in the sample.

- Arithmetic mean rigidly defined by Algebric Formula
- It is easy to calculate and simple to understand
- It is based on all observations and it can be regarded as representative of the given data

• It is capable of being treated mathematically and hence it is widely used in statistical analysis.

• Arithmetic mean can be computed even if the detailed distribution is not known but some of the observation and number of the observation are known.

• It is least affected by the fluctuation of sampling

Disadvantages of Arithmetic Mean

• It can neither be determined by inspection or by graphical location

• Arithmetic mean cannot be computed for qualitative data like data on intelligence honesty and smoking habit etc

• It is too much affected by extreme observations and hence it is not adequately represent data consisting of some extreme point

• Arithmetic mean cannot be computed when class intervals have open ends.

MEDIAN

The median is that value of the series which divides the group into two equal parts, one part comprising all values greater than the median value and the other part comprising all the values smaller than the median value.

Advantages of Median

(1) Simplicity: It is very simple measure of the central tendency of the series. I the case of simple statistical series, just a glance at the data is enough to locate the median value.

(2) Free from the effect of extreme values: Unlike arithmetic mean, median value is not destroyed by the extreme values of the series.

(3) Certainty: Certainty is another merits is the median. Median values are always a certain specific value in the series.

(4) Real value: Median value is real value and is a better representative value of the series compared to arithmetic mean average, the value of which may not exist in the series at all.

(5) Graphic presentation: Besides algebraic approach, the median value can be estimated also through the graphic presentation of data.

(6) Possible even when data is incomplete: Median can be estimated even in the case of certain incomplete series. It is enough if one knows the number of items and the middle item of the series.

Disadvantages of Median

Following are the various demerits of median:

(1) Lack of representative character: Median fails to be a representative measure in case of such series the different values of which are wide apart from each other. Also, median is of limited representative character as it is not based on all the items in the series.

(2) Unrealistic: When the median is located somewhere between the two middle values, it remains only an approximate measure, not a precise value.

(3) Lack of Algebraic Treatment: Arithmetic mean is capable of further algebraic treatment, but median is not. For example, multiplying the median with the number of items in the series will not give us the sum total of the values of the series.

However, median is quite a simple method finding an average of a series. It is quite a commonly used measure in the case of such series which are related to qualitative observation as and health of the student.

MODE

The value of the variable which occurs most frequently in a distribution is called the mode.

Advantages of Mode

Following are the various advantages of mode:

(1) Simple and popular: Mode is very simple measure of central tendency. Sometimes, just at the series is enough to locate the model value. Because of its simplicity, it s a very popular measure of the central tendency.

(2) Less effect of marginal values: Compared top mean, mode is less affected by marginal values in the series. Mode is determined only by the value with highest frequencies.

(3) Graphic presentation: Mode can be located graphically, with the help of histogram.

(4) Best representative: Mode is that value which occurs most frequently in the series. Accordingly, mode is the best representative value of the series.

(5) No need of knowing all the items or frequencies: The calculation of mode does not require knowledge of all the items and frequencies of a distribution. In simple series, it is enough if one knows the items with highest frequencies in the distribution.

Disadvantages of Mode:

Following are the various demerits of mode:

(1) Uncertain and vague: Mode is an uncertain and vague measure of the central tendency.

(2) Not capable of algebraic treatment: Unlike mean, mode is not capable of further algebraic treatment.

(3) Difficult: With frequencies of all items are identical, it is difficult to identify the modal value.

(4) Complex procedure of grouping: Calculation of mode involves cumbersome procedure of grouping the data. If the extent of grouping changes there will be a change in the model value.

(5) Ignores extreme marginal frequencies: It ignores extreme marginal frequencies. To that extent model value is not a representative value of all the items in a series. Besides, one can question the representative character of the model value as its calculation does not involve all items of the series.

15

Measures of Variability: Meaning, Importance, Computing from Group and Ungroup Data

MEASURES OF CENTRAL TENDENCY

Measures of average such as the median and mean represent the typical value for a dataset. Within the dataset the actual values usually differ from one another and from the average value itself. The extent to which the median and mean are good representatives of the values in the original dataset depends upon the variability or dispersion in the original data. Datasets are said to have high dispersion when they contain values considerably higher and lower than the mean value.

In Figure 2 the number of different sized tutorial groups in semester 1 and semester 2 are presented. In both semesters the mean and median tutorial group size is 5 students, however the groups in semester 2 show more dispersion (or variability in size) than those in semester 1.

Figure 1: Comparison of Tutorial Group Sizes

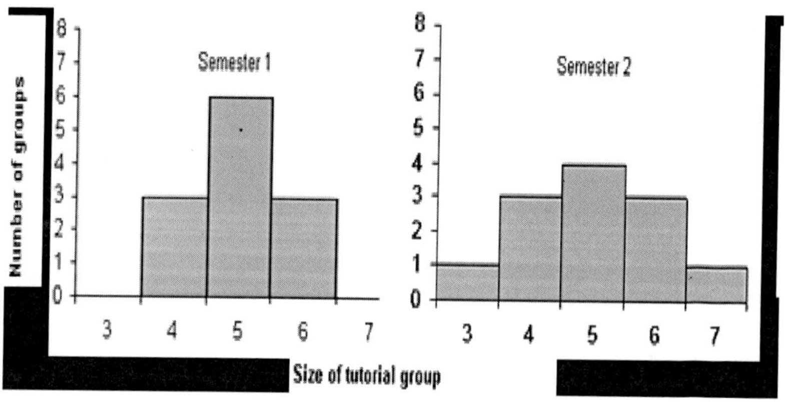

Dispersion within a dataset can be measured or described in several ways including the range, inter-quartile range and standard deviation.

THE RANGE

The range is the most obvious measure of dispersion and is the difference between the lowest and highest values in a dataset. In Figure 1, the size of the largest semester 1 tutorial group is 6 students and the size of the smallest group is 4 students, resulting in a range of 2 (6-4). In semester 2, the largest tutorial group size is 7 students and the smallest tutorial group contains 3 students, therefore the range is 4 (7-3).

The range is simple to compute and is useful when you wish to evaluate the whole of a dataset.

The range is useful for showing the spread within a dataset and for comparing the spread between similar datasets.

An example of the use of the range to compare spread within datasets is provided in Table 1. The scores of individual students in the examination and coursework component of a module are shown.

Table 1: Comparison of cousework and examination marks of 14 students

Student	A	B	C	D	E	F	G	H	I	J	K	L	M	N
Coursework mark	27	44	39	23	41	48	37	34	40	43	30	43	29	27
Examination mark	12	47	26	25	38	45	35	35	41	39	32	25	18	30

To find the range in marks the highest and lowest values need to be found from the table. The highest coursework mark was 48 and the lowest was 27 giving a range of 21. In the examination, the highest mark was 45 and the lowest 12 producing a range of 33. This indicates that there was wider variation in the students' performance in the examination than in the coursework for this module.

Since the range is based solely on the two most extreme values within the dataset, if one of these is either exceptionally high or low (sometimes referred to as outlier) it will result in a range that is not typical of the variability within the dataset. For example, imagine in the above example that one student failed to hand in any coursework and was awarded a mark of zero, however they sat the exam and scored 40. The range for the coursework marks would now become 48 (48-0), rather than 21, however the new range is not typical of the dataset as a whole and is distorted by the outlier in the coursework marks. In order to reduce the problems caused by outliers in a dataset, the inter-quartile range is often calculated instead of the range.

The Inter-quartile Range

The inter-quartile range is a measure that indicates the extent to which the central 50% of values within the dataset are dispersed. It is based upon, and related to, the median.

In the same way that the median divides a dataset into two halves, it can be further divided into quarters by identifying the upper and lower quartiles. The lower quartile is found one quarter of the way along a dataset when the values have been arranged in order of magnitude; the upper quartile is found three quarters along the dataset. Therefore, the upper quartile lies half way between the median and the highest value in the dataset whilst the lower quartile lies halfway between the median and the lowest value in the dataset. The inter-quartile range is found by subtracting the lower quartile from the upper quartile.

For example, the examination marks for 20 students following a particular module are arranged in order of magnitude.

Lower quartile (E–F) Median (J–K) Upper quartile (O–P)

Student	A	B	C	D	E	F	G	H	I	J	K	L	M	N	O	P	Q	R	S	T
Mark	43	48	50	50	52	53	56	58	59	60	62	65	68	68	70	71	74	76	78	80

The median lies at the mid-point between the two central values (10th and 11th)

= half-way between 60 and 62 = 61

The lower quartile lies at the mid-point between the 5th and 6th values

= half-way between 52 and 53 = 52.5

The upper quartile lies at the mid-point between the 15th and 16th values

= half-way between 70 and 71 = 70.5

The inter-quartile range for this dataset is therefore 70.5 - 52.5 = 18 whereas the range is: 80 - 43 = 37.

The inter-quartile range provides a clearer picture of the overall dataset by removing/ignoring the outlying values.

Like the range however, the inter-quartile range is a measure of dispersion that is based upon only two values from the dataset. Statistically, the standard deviation is a more powerful measure of dispersion because it takes into account every value in the dataset. The standard deviation is explored in the next section of this guide.

Calculating the Inter-quartile range using Excel

The method Excel uses to calculate quartiles is not commonly used and tends to produce unusual results particularly when the dataset contains only a few values. For this reason you may be best to calculate the inter-quartile range by hand.

THE STANDARD DEVIATION

The standard deviation is a measure that summarises the amount by which every value within a dataset varies from the mean. Effectively it indicates how tightly the values in the dataset are bunched around the mean value. It is the most robust and widely used measure of dispersion since, unlike the range and inter-quartile range, it takes into account every variable in the dataset. When the values in a dataset are pretty tightly bunched together the standard deviation is small. When the values are spread apart the standard deviation will be relatively large. The standard deviation is usually presented in conjunction with the mean and is measured in the same units.

In many datasets the values deviate from the mean value due to chance and such datasets are said to display a normal distribution. In a dataset with a normal distribution most of the values are clustered around the mean while relatively few values tend to be extremely high or extremely low. Many natural phenomena display a normal distribution.

For datasets that have a normal distribution the standard deviation can be used to determine the proportion of values that lie within a particular range of the mean value. For such distributions it is always the case that 68% of values are less than one standard deviation (1SD) away from the mean value, that 95% of values are less than two standard deviations (2SD) away from the mean and that 99% of values are less than three standard deviations (3SD) away from the mean. Figure 2 shows this concept in diagrammatical form.

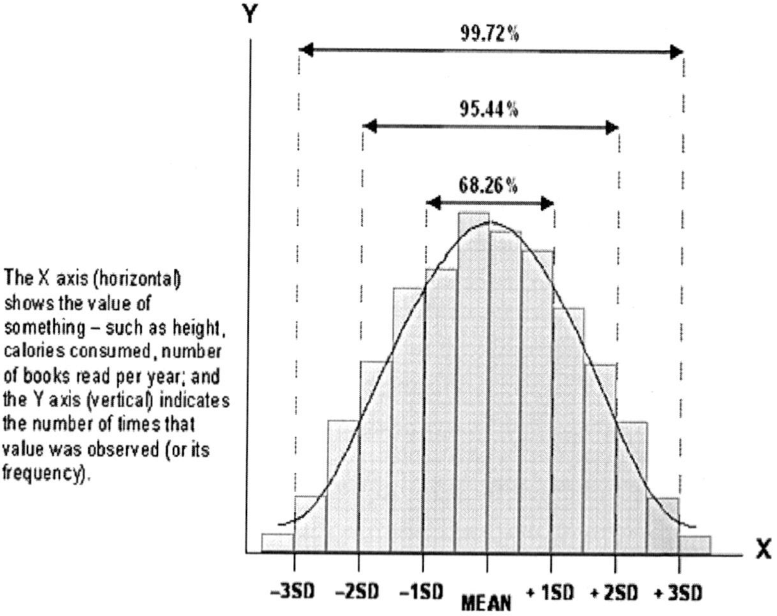

Figure 2

If the mean of a dataset is 25 and its standard deviation is 1.6, then 68% of the values in the dataset will lie between MEAN-1SD (25-1.6=23.4) and MEAN+1SD (25+1.6=26.6) 99% of the values will lie between MEAN-3SD (25-4.8=20.2) and MEAN+3SD (25+4.8=29.8).

If the dataset had the same mean of 25 but a larger standard deviation (for example, 2.3) it would indicate that the values were more dispersed. The frequency distribution for a dispersed dataset would still show a normal distribution but when plotted on a graph the shape of the curve will be flatter as in Figure 3.

SAMPLE STANDARD DEVIATIONS

There are two different calculations for the Standard Deviation. Which formula you use depends upon whether the values in your dataset represent an entire population or whether they form a sample of a larger population. For example, if all student users of the library were asked how many books they had borrowed in the past month then the entire population has been studied since all the students have been asked. In such cases the population standard deviation should be used. Sometimes it is not possible to find information about an entire population and it might be more realistic to ask a sample of 150 students about their library borrowing and use these results to estimate library borrowing habits for the entire population of students. In such cases the sample standard deviation should be used.

Formulae for the standard deviation

Whilst it is not necessary to learn the formula for calculating the standard deviation, there may be times when you wish to include it in a report or dissertation.

The standard deviation of an entire population is known as σ (sigma) and is calculated using:

Where x represents each value in the population, μ is the mean value of the population, is the summation (or total), and N is the number of values in the population.

$$\frac{\sum (x-\mu)^2}{N}$$

The standard deviation of a sample is known as S and is calculated using:

Example 4: Typical frequency distributions for clustered and dispersed datasets

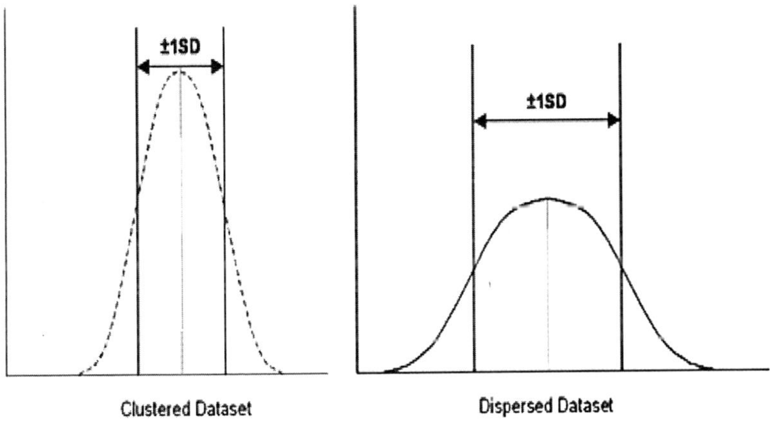

Figure 3

Where x represents each value in the population, x is the mean value of the sample, Σ is the summation (or total), and n-1 is the number of values in the sample minus 1.

MEASURES OF VARIABILITY—GROUPED DATA

As for the case of ungrouped data there are two measures of variability for grouped data: the variance and standard deviation. The definition is very similar to that of ungrouped data, except this time we use the midpoints again as we did for the mean. We therefore have the following results...

Population Variance and Standard Deviation

Original Formula

Computational Formula

$$\sigma^2 = \frac{\Sigma fM^2 - \frac{(\Sigma fM)^2}{N}}{N}$$

where

- f = the frequency
- M = class midpoint
- N = sum of all frequencies

SAMPLE VARIANCE AND STANDARD DEVIATION

Original Formula

$$s^2 = \frac{\Sigma f(M - \overline{x})^2}{n-1}$$

Computational Formula

$$s^2 = \frac{\Sigma fM^2 - \frac{(\Sigma fM)^2}{n}}{n-1}$$

where

- f = the frequency
- M = class midpoint
- n = sum of all frequencies
- $\bar{x}$ = grouped mean for the population

Example

You are given the times of when goals were scored in the Premier League last season:

Time	Frequency
0-15134	
15-30	146
30-45	184
45-60	173
60-75	191
75-90	238

and you are required to calculate the standard deviation of the data.

Time	Frequency	Midpoint	Frequency × Midpoint	(M - Mean)	(M - Mean)^2	Frequency × (M – Mean)^2
0-15	134	7.5	1005	-42.03	1766.60	236724.58
15-30	146	22.5	3285	-27.03	730.67	106679.20
30-45	184	37.5	6900	-12.03	144.74	26632.88
45-60	173	52.5	9083	2.97	8.82	1525.03
60-75	191	67.5	12893	17.97	322.89	61671.32
75-90	238	82.5	19635	32.97	1086.96	258695.96
	1066		**52800**			**691927.98**

We therefore find that

$$Variance - \frac{\Sigma f(M-\mu)^2}{\Sigma f} = \frac{691927.9784}{1066} = 649.09$$

and

$$\text{Standard deviation} = \sqrt{649.09} = 25.5$$

Mean for Grouped Data

To calculate the mean for grouped data, first find the midpoint of each class and then multiply the midpoint by the frequencies of the corresponding classes. The sum of these products gives an approximation for the sum of all values. To find the value of mean, divide this sum by the total number of observations in the data. The formulas used to calculate the mean for grouped data are as follows:

Mean for population data: $\mu = \frac{\Sigma mf}{N}$

Mean for sample data : $\bar{x} = \frac{\Sigma mf}{N}$

where m is the midpoint and f is the frequency of a class.

Variance and Standard Deviation for Grouped Data

Following are the basic formulas used to calculate the population and sample variances for grouped data.

$$\sigma^2 = \frac{\Sigma f(m-\mu)^2}{N} \text{ and } s^2 = \frac{\Sigma f(m-\bar{x})^2}{n-1}$$

where σ^2 is the population variance, s^2 is the sample variance and m is the midpoint of a class.

In either cases, the standard deviation is obtained by taking the positive square root of the variance.

Again, the following computational formulas are more efficient for calculating the variance and standard deviation.

$$\sigma^2 = \frac{\Sigma m^2 f - \frac{(\Sigma mf)^2}{N}}{N} \text{ and } s^2 = \frac{\Sigma m^2 f - \frac{(\Sigma mf)^2}{n}}{n-1}$$

where σ^2 is the population variance, s^2 is the sample variance and m is the midpoint of a class. The standard deviation is obtained by taking the positive square root of the variance.

The population standard deviation: $\sigma = \sqrt{\sigma^2}$

The sample standard deviation: $s = \sqrt{s^2}$

16

Percentiles and Quartiles: Meaning, Importance, Computing from Group and Ungroup Data

PERCENTILE

A percentile is a measure at which that percentage of the total values are the same as or below that measure. For example, 90% of the data values lie below the 90th percentile, whereas 10% of the data values lie below the 10th percentile.

The nth percentile of a set of data is the value at which n% of the data is below it. Percentiles generalize the idea of a quartile and allow us to split our data set into many pieces. We will examine percentiles and learn more about their connections to other topics in statistics.

Quartiles and Percentiles

Given a data set that has been ordered in increasing magnitude, the median, first quartile and third quartile can be used split the data into four pieces. The first quartile is the point at which one fourth of the data lies below it. The median is located exactly in the middle of the data set, with half of all of the data below it. The third quartile is the place where three fourths of the data lies below it.

The median, first quartile and third quartile can all be stated in terms of percentiles. Since half of the data is less than the median, and one half is equal to 50%, we could call the median the 50th percentile. One fourth is equal to 25%, and so the first quartile the 25th percentile.

An Example of a Percentile

A class of 20 students had the following scores on their most recent test: 75, 77, 78, 78, 80, 81, 81, 82, 83, 84, 84, 84, 85, 87, 87, 88, 88, 88, 89, 90. The score of 80% has four scores below it. Since 4/20 = 20%, 80 is the 20th percentile of the class. The score of 90 has 19 scores below it. Since 19/20 = 95%, 90 corresponds to the 95 percentile of the class.

Percentile vs. Percentage

Be careful with the words percentile and percentage. A percentage score indicates the proportion of a test that someone has completed correctly. A percentile score tells us what percent of other scores are less than the data point we are investigating. As seen in the above example these numbers are rarely the same.

Deciles and Percentiles

Besides quartiles, a fairly common way to arrange a set of data is by deciles. A decile has the same root word as decimal and so it makes sense that each decile serves as a demarcation of 10% of a set of data. This means that the first decile is the 10th percentile. The second decile is the 20th percentile. Deciles provide a way to split a data set into more pieces than quartiles without splitting it into 100 pieces as with percentiles.

Applications of Percentiles

Percentile scores have a variety of uses. Anytime that a set of data needs to be broken into digestible chunks, percentiles are helpful. One common application of percentiles is for use with tests, such as the SAT, to serve as a basis of comparison for those who took the test. In the above example, a score of 80% initially sounds good. However this does not sound as impressive when we find out that it is the 20th percentile - only 20% of the class scored less than an 80% on the test.

Another example of percentiles being used are in children's growth charts. In addition to a physical height or weight measurement, pediatricians typically state this in terms of a percentile score. A percentile is used in this situation in order to compare the height or weight of a given child to all children of that age. This allows for an effective means of comparison.

QUARTILES

Quartiles are values that divide a (part of a) data table into four groups containing an approximately equal number of observations. The total of 100% is split into four equal parts: 25%, 50%, 75% and 100%.

The first quartile (or lower quartile), Q1, is defined as the value that has an f-value equal to 0.25. This is the same thing as the twenty-fifth percentile. The third quartile (or upper quartile), Q3, has an f-value equal to 0.75. The interquartile range, IQR, is defined as Q3-Q1.

- **The percentiles and quartiles are computed as follows:**

1. The f-value of each value in the data table is computed:

$$f_i = \frac{i-1}{n-1}$$

where i is the index of the value, and n the number of values.

2. The first quartile is computed by interpolating between the f-values immediately below and above 0.25, to arrive at the value corresponding to the f-value 0.25.

3. The third quartile is computed by interpolating between the f-values immediately below and above 0.75, to arrive at the value corresponding to the f-value 0.75.

4. Any other percentile is similarly calculated by interpolating between the appropriate values.

Examples:

Value	f-value
4	0
8	0.2
9	0.4
11	0.6
16	
0.8	
17	
1.0	

Interpolation at f-value=0.75 yields Q3=14.75.

Describing other locations in a distribution

The mean and median both describe the 'centre' of a distribution. This is usually what you want to summarise about a set of marks, but occasionally a different part of the distribution is of more interest.

For example, you might want to describe a typical mark for a 'good' or 'weak' student.

Quartiles

The median of a distribution splits the data into two equally-sized groups. In the same way, the quartiles are the three values that split a data set into four equal parts. Note that the 'middle' quartile is the median.

The upper quartile describes a 'typical' mark for the top half of a class and the lower quartile is a 'typical' mark for the bottom half of the class.

The quartiles are closely related to the histogram of a data set. Since area equals the proportion of values in a histogram, the quartiles split the histogram into four approximately equal areas.

(The relationship is only approximate if the quartiles do not coincide with histogram bin boundaries.)

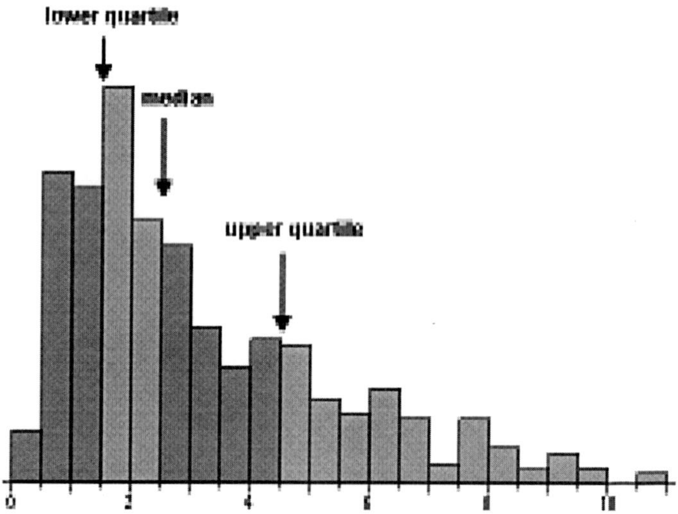

Deciles

In a similar way, the deciles of a distribution are the nine values that split the data set into ten equal parts.

You should not try to calculate deciles from small data sets -- a single class of marks is too small to get useful values since the extreme deciles are very variable. However the deciles can be useful descriptions for larger data sets such as national distributions for marks from standard tests.

The diagram below shows a jittered dot plot of 60 marks from an exam.

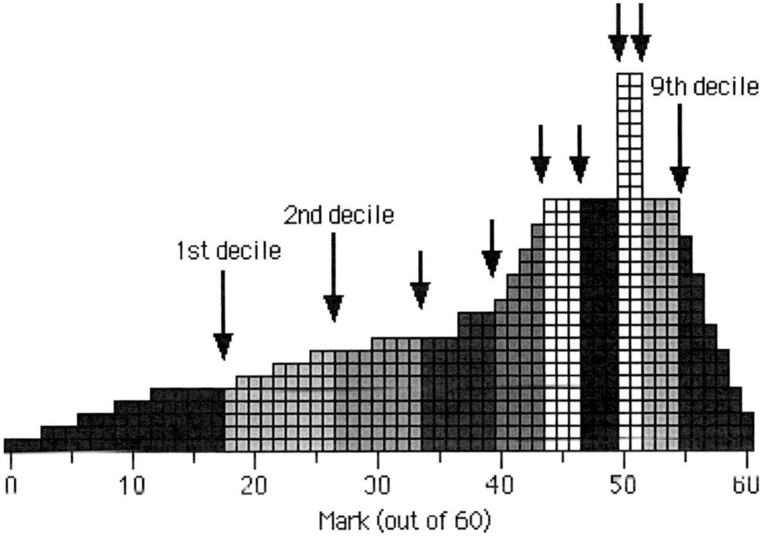

Use the pop-up menu to display deciles for the data, and verify that the 9 deciles split the students into 10 groups, each containing 6 students.

Deciles for the distribution and for individual students

The term 'decile' is used in two different contexts. It is confusing that the same word is used in both ways, so be careful!

When applied to a distribution (a large group of marks), there are nine deciles, each of which is a mark.

A student whose mark is below the first decile is said to be in decile 1. Similarly, a student whose marks is between the first and second deciles is in decile 2, ... and a student whose marks is above the ninth decile is in decile 10. When applied to individual students, the term 'decile' is therefore a number between 1 and 10.

For example, the histogram below shows the distribution of marks in a test (out of 60) that was attempted by 600 students. Each student's mark is represented by a square in the histogram.

The nine deciles split the students into 10 groups of 60.

The first decile is 17.5 so the weakest tenth of the students in the class had a mark below this. This decile therefore summarises the performance of the weakest students.

Students with marks below 17.5 are said to be in decile 1. Those with marks between 17.5 and 26.5 are in decile 2, and so on, up to students with marks higher than 54.5 who are in decile 10.

Details

Unfortunately there is no commonly accepted precise definition for the lower and upper quartiles -- different software (and indeed different statisticians!) use slightly different values. One simple definition is that the lower quartile is the median of the lower half of the data (excluding the middle value if there is an even number of values) with a similar definition for the upper quartile.

In practice, the precise definition is of little practical importance, especially for large data sets. The main thing to remember is to be consistent with your definition if you are comparing several data sets.

There are similar problems with precisely defining deciles but again the precise definition used should not affect your interpretation of the data.

In practice, you are advised to use the functions built into Excel to evaluate quartiles and deciles.

Percentiles

In a similar way, the percentiles of a distribution are the 99 values that split the data set into a hundred equal parts. These percentiles can be used to categorise the individuals into percentile 1, ..., percentile 100.

A very large data set is required before the extreme percentiles can be estimated with any accuracy. (The 'random' variability in marks is especially noticeable in the extremes of a data set.)

IMPORTANCE OF PERCENTILE

A percentile (or a centile) is a measure used in statistics indicating the value below which a given percentage of observations in a group of observations fall. For example, the 20th percentile is the value (or score) below which 20% of the observations may be found.

Percentiles report the relative standing of a particular value within a statistical data set. If that's what you're most interested in, the actual mean and standard deviation of the data set are not important, and neither is the actual data value. What's important is where you stand — not in relation to the mean, but in relation to everyone else: That's what a percentile gives you.

For example, in the case of exam scores, who cares what the mean is, as long as you scored better than most of the class? Who knows, it may have been an impossible exam and 40 points out of 100 was a great score. In this case, your score itself is meaningless, but your percentile tells you everything.

Suppose your exam score is better than 90% of the rest of the class. That means your exam score is at the 90th percentile (so k = 90), which hopefully gets you an A. Conversely, if your score is at the 10th percentile (which would never happen to you, because you're such an excellent student), then k = 10; that means only 10% of the other scores are below yours, and 90% of them are above yours; in this case an A is not in your future.

A nice property of percentiles is they have a universal interpretation: Being at the 95th percentile means the same thing no matter if you are looking at exam scores or weights of packages sent through the postal service; the 95th percentile always means 95% of the other values lie below yours, and 5% lie above it. This also allows you to fairly compare two data sets that have different means and standard deviations (like ACT scores in reading versus math). It evens the playing field and gives you a way to compare apples to oranges, so to speak.

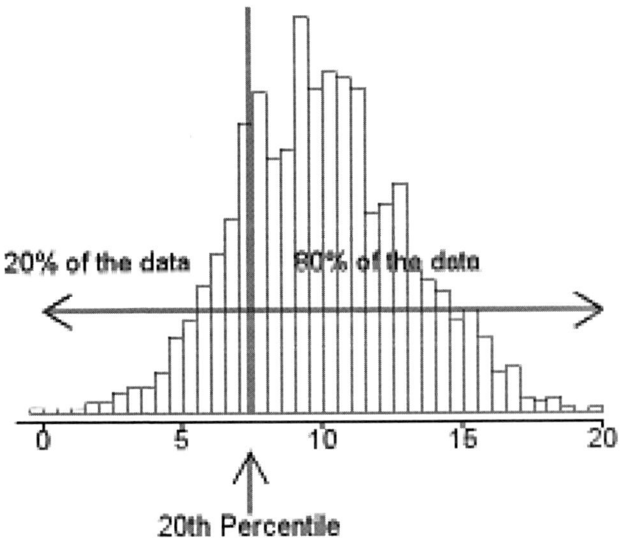

"Percentile" is in everyday used, but there is no universal definition for it. The most common definition of a percentile is a number where a certain percentage of scores fall below that percentile. You might know that you scored 67 out of 90 on a test. But that figure has no real meaning unless you know what percentile you fall into. If you know that your score is in the 90th percentile, that means you scored better than 90% of people who took the test.

Percentiles are commonly used to report scores in tests, like the SAT, GRE and LSAT. for example, the 70th percentile on the 2013 GRE was 156. That means if you scored 156 on the exam, your score was better than 70 percent of test takers.

The word "percentile" is used informally in the above definition. In common use, the percentile usually indicates that a certain percentage falls below that percentile. For example, if you score in the 25th percentile, then 25% of test takers are below your score. The "25" is called the percentile rank. In statistics, it can get a little more complicated as there are actually three definitions of "percentile." Here are the first two (see below for definition 3), based on an arbitrary "25th percentile":

Definition 1: The nth percentile is the lowest score that is greater than a certain percentage ("n") of the scores. In this example, our n is 25, so we're looking for the lowest score that is greater than 25%.

Definition 2: The nth percentile is the smallest score that is greater than or equal to a certain percentage of the scores. To rephrase this, it's the percentage of data that falls at or below a certain observation. This is the definition used in AP statistics. In this example, the 25th percentile is the score that's greater or equal to 25% of the scores.

How to Find a Percentile?

Sample question: Find out where the 25th percentile is in the above list.

Step 1: Calculate what rank is at the 25th percentile. Use the following formula:

Rank = Percentile / 100 * (number of items + 1)

Rank = 25 / 100 * (8 + 1) = 0.25 * 9 = 2.25.

A rank of 2.25 is at the 25th percentile. However, there isn't a rank of 2.25 (ever heard of a high school rank of 2.25? I haven't!), so you must either round up, or round down. As 2.25 is closer to 2 than 3, I'm going to round down to a rank of 2.

Step 2: Choose either definition 1 or 2:

Definition 1: The lowest score that is greater than 25% of the scores. That equals a score of 43 on this list (a rank of 3).

Definition 2: The smallest score that is greater than or equal to 25% of the scores. That equals a score of 33 on this list (a rank of 2).

Depending on which definition you use, the 25th percentile could be reported at 33 or 43! A third definition attempts to correct this possible misinterpretation:

Definition 3: A weighted mean of the percentiles from the first two definitions.

In the above example, here's how the percentile would be worked out using the weighted mean:

Multiply the difference between the scores by 0.25 (the fraction of the rank we calculated above). The scores were 43 and 33, giving us a difference of 10:

(0.25)(43 – 33) = 2.5

Add the result to the lower score. 2.5 + 33 = 35.5

In this case, the 25th percentile score is 35.5, which makes more sense as it's in the middle of 43 and 33.

In most cases, the percentile is usually definition #1. However, it would be wise to double check that any statistics about percentiles are created using that first definition.

4. Percentile Range

A percentile range is the difference between two specified percentiles. these could theoretically be any two percentiles, but the 10-90 percentile range is the most common. To find the 10-90 percentile range:

Calculate the 10th percentile using the above steps.

Calculate the 90th percentile using the above steps.

Subtract Step 1 (the 10th percentile) from Step 2 (the 90th percentile).

IMPORTANCE OF QUARTILE

Quartile is a useful concept in statistics and is conceptually similar to the median. The first quartile is the data point at the 25th percentile, and the third quartile is the data point at the 75th percentile. The 50th percentile is the median.

To understand a quartile, let us revisit median. To compute the median, we cut off the data into two groups with equal number of points. Thus the middle value that separates these groups is the median. In a similar fashion, if we divide the data into 4 equal groups now instead of 2, the first differentiating point is the first quartile, the second differentiating point is the second quartile which is the same as the median and the third such differentiating point is the third quartile.

To further see what quartiles do, the first quartile is at the 25th percentile. This means that 25% of the data is smaller than the first quartile and 75% of the data is larger than this. Similarly, in case of the third quartile, 25% of the data is larger than it while 75% of it is smaller. For the second quartile, which is nothing but the median, 50% or half of the data is smaller while half of the data is larger than this value.

Interpreting Quartiles

As you know, the median is a measure of the central tendency of the data but says nothing about how the data is distributed in the two arms on either side of the median. Quartiles help us measure this.

Thus if the first quartile is far away from the median while the third quartile is closer to it, it means that the data points that are smaller than the median are spread far apart while the data points that are greater than the median are closely packed together.

An Alternative View

Another way of understanding quartiles is by thinking of those as medians of either of the two sets of data points differentiated by the median. In this case, the first quartile is the median of the data that is smaller than the full median while the third quartile is the median of the data that is larger than the full median. Here full median is used in the context of the median of the entire set of data.

It should be noted that a quartile is not limited to discrete variables but also applies equally well to continuous variables. In this case, you will need to know the data distribution to figure out the quartiles. If the distribution is symmetric, like normal distribution, then the first and third quartiles are equidistant from the median in either direction.

Selected References

Cochran, W.G., and Cox, G.M. *Experimental Designs*. New York: John Wiley & Sons, 1957.

Finney, D.J. *An Introduction to the Theory of Experimental Design.* Chicago: University of Chicago Press, 1960.

Kempthorne, Oscar. *The Design and Analysis of Experiments.* New York: John Wiley & Sons, 1952.

Rothstein, Anne L.,*Research Design and Statistics for Physical Education.* Prentice-Hall, Inc., Englewood Cliffs,N.J. 1985.

Scheffe, H. *Analysis of Variance.* New York: John Wiley & Sons, 1959.

Searle, S.R. *Linear Models*. New York: John Wiley & Sons, 1971.

Verma, J.P., *A Textbook on Sports Statistics,* Sports Publication, New Delhi.

Shaw, Dhananjoy, *Fundamental Statistics in Physical Education and Sports Sciences,* 1998, Sports Publication, New Delhi.

Singh, Lakhwinder, Sharma, Ved Parkash, Rai Vaibhav, *Statistics in Physical Education,* Khel Sahitya Kendra, New Delhi.